The Recollections Of An Accidental Polymath

Dave Gibbons

An Accidental Polymath

Published by Amazon for Dave Gibbons

© Copyright 2021

ISBN: 9798742545064

The Recollections Of
An Accidental Polymath

Disclaimer - please read first!

What follows is an account of a variety of events that have occurred during my life so far. Some may be of interest, others not. There will be those of you reading this mentioned by name, and stories told about us and my memories of you. These are my recollections and anecdotes, and I'm sure you may have a completely different view on how things went at the time, so I apologise if things don't quite tally.

Writing this has been a cathartic and exposing process, and has on occasion reminded me that sometimes, I was not a very nice person - please don't judge too harshly.

I've endeavoured to not be defamatory to anyone, and hope that I've succeeded, my purpose was not to offend in any way. Please take the words on these pages in the spirit in which I wrote them.

Be advised that there will be a little repetition, as there are overlaps of time in some of the stories, I've written this such that each chapter could be read independently. Or not if you so wish.

There is no story of triumph over adversity, or challenges overcome. These are just the stories of some of the things that I've managed to cram into my life so far.

If you are one of the people mentioned in the following pages, thank you for being part of my varied life. All of you have made my life richer in one way or another.

Dedicated to

Scott

Grasp every opportunity and try everything (but not drugs)

and

Alli

There's no I in team, but there's always been a you

Thanks to

Olivia Eisinger

Olivia is a professional editor, and in her wisdom removed from the 'stream of consciousness' that I gave her, all the contentious language and inferences that otherwise would have landed me in a whole heap of trouble had it been published!

oliviaeisinger@icloud.com

and

Russ Smith

Russ is also a professional editor, and as you will read in the following pages gave me my first opportunity to 'write out loud'. He very graciously offered to give the edited manuscript a final read through in case Olivia and I had missed something.

Contents

An Accidental Polymath

Foreword

I guess it's true to say Dave and I have known one another for 40 years.

The reason? I started work as a Trainee Commentator in early 1981 at Santa Pod Raceway and, an already established star in the field of Competition Altereds was, the man himself.

I don't remember (sign of my age) exactly how Dave, his Crew Chief, Dick Hogben and I met up and became friends. To me – it just sort of happened.

Dave and the team were always good at what they did, and were always in the thick of the Altered battles, whether it was against Herb Andrews (Magnum Force), or Team Paranoia (Brian and Alan), it was always exciting to watch and led to me learn, quite quickly, about a sport I had never in my life, watched before.

I was driving a Bull Nose Firebird at the time, and although it was a beautiful car (how I wish I had it now!), it wouldn't control the quite heavy 4-wheel trailer I had, which housed all my disco equipment. Driving to Bristol from Kent at 40 miles per hour wasn't fun!

So whilst discussing this with Dave and Dick, they decided the best course of action for me was to swop my Firebird for Dick's El Camino pick-up truck (how I wish I still had that too!).

How right they were… Suddenly, driving to gigs was a pleasure if not always at the speed limit, and when it went wrong (only once in all the time I had it), who fixed it? Yup - Dave and Dick.

So here he was – this little man with a nearly permanent moustache who could race, fix cars, entertain and was a great friend. (His Mum used to phone me in my office to talk about insurance, and when asked who was calling, she used to say to the receptionist, 'Tell him it's his other Mummy!!' - I must have been over 40 at that time!

Now he is a self-employed engineer, an actor, and a celebrant, but still most importantly, an entertainer and a friend.

Enjoy the ups and downs of this book about his life story – I laughed my way through it and had a tear in my eye at the appropriate time.

Long live Funky Gibbons/Dee Gee/Gibb/Sweet Cheeks/Manuel or what other name he may go by.

John Price

Prologue

I drove into the metal stockholders' yard, down a pot-holed road on a farm yard around the back of the golf club in Woodmansterne. I'd been a customer for at least fifteen years, and the proprietor Les was seated behind his desk as usual. He was a stocky bloke, bearded and ginger with a fondness for rugby, and probably ten years my senior. There was always some banter between us, but this day our discussion led to me revealing some of the things I did to earn a crust.

'You're a bit of a polymath!' he said.

I wasn't sure whether to kiss him or punch him in the mouth! I chose not to do either, complete our business and go home and look up the word 'polymath'.

Definition of a polymath:

Noun:

"A person of great and varied learning"

(*Collins English Dictionary*)

So yes, it turns out that I am indeed a bit of a polymath, or perhaps even a lot of one. As mentioned above, the dictionary-definition is 'a person of great and varied learning', to which I choose to interpret as someone who has a good deal of experience in a variety of areas. As I reflect in my sixty-fourth year, it's fair to say that I have experienced a great deal of 'stuff' in my life.

I've never had any sort of life plan, I've pretty much allowed life to happen to me sort of by accident, and frankly I've managed to get away with it – and still do! Mum often said that I led a charmed life, perhaps that's true. She was a young woman during the Second World War, worked hard and saw hardship, as had my father. I've had it dead easy by comparison.

My parents encouraged me to try anything and everything (although in spite of my mother's best efforts I remain a fussy eater to this day), and gave me as many opportunities as their income would allow. We were not a wealthy family, but my father made a good job of making it appear that we were better off than we actually were.

I realised a little over a year ago that I'd managed to do quite a lot of 'stuff' during my years. I never anticipated that my father would die, and failed to ask him enough questions before he passed, and figured the same thing may well happen with my own son. So, I wrote this as a legacy for him and all that may follow, but having done so now, I think that it may be something I should share more widely.

My hope is that these pages may fill in some of the gaps in what is known about Dave Gibbons. If you are not my son and reading this, there's a good chance you know me, and will be aware of much of what I write, but perhaps discover some things you didn't know. If you are a stranger, then thank you for taking the time to look at my ramblings. It's not my intention to educate, or imbue any great message. There are no lessons to be learnt, I simply aim to share, amuse and delight.

I don't have a story about any sort of struggle to get by, or get along – these are recollections of my life written for no other reasons than my own satisfaction and more importantly, to allow my son to learn about me, my background, and my life.

Expect references to cars... My life has been pretty much inextricably linked to cars and motorsport, so much of what I remember will be because a car I was driving at the time sparks the memory.

So here we go, the recollections of 'an accidental polymath'.

1

From fields of mint and lavender

The St. Helier Estate was built during the late 1920s and early 1930s by the London County Council to satisfy the demands of a post-First World War population on a decaying city centre. Named after LCC Alderman Lady St. Helier, it was built on an area known for both lavender and mint and sat on land in Sutton, Mitcham, Morden and Carshalton and was within both the London boroughs of Sutton and Merton. It was one of the largest new housing developments ever undertaken. I recall that up until the mid-70s some areas still had 'pre-fab' houses erected during WW2 to provide emergency housing, but these small single-storey homes were principally made from asbestos - so they had to go.

I was born in the St. Helier Hospital on the 19th January 1957 to Reginald Percy and Doreen Mary Gibbons, and my wife and son were both born in the same hospital. I'm sure more well-known people were born there too, and future Conservative Prime Minister John Major was just one of them. At the time, my parents lived in one of the two-up two-down same-as-everybody-else's-houses on the estate in Muchelney Road. This road differed slightly from the rest of the estate as it faced a patch of green with some trees - a much nicer outlook than another brick-built house. My dad's parents, Walter and Amy (Nan and Pop-pop to me), lived in an identical house on Bishopsford Road, running parallel.

Grandad was a soldier, and married Nan during the First World War – six months before giving birth to their first child, so it doesn't take a genius to work out why they got married. The daughter was named Amy – the same as her mum (so not a great deal of imagination involved) but grew up to be known by everyone as Golly. My maternal grandmother frowned upon the relationship between my Dad and Mum, saying that she 'Didn't want her daughter going out with that Jewish boy'. This was confusing to me as we were clearly not of Jewish faith, until I discovered that my Nan's maiden name was Yendall. That name was a bit of a clue.

They'd all moved in from Earlsfield which was not far away on the other side of Tooting. Pop-pop ran a greengrocers' shop in Garratt Lane, and he and Nan raised four boys and two girls - my dad being the second oldest of the boys. Where Dad's brothers and sisters were living at the time I have no idea.

(Originally coming from Bristol, in the early 1900s the Gibbons family hailed from Lambeth and then moved to Earlsfield, so on the cusp of being cockneys but definitely from 'Sarf' London. Ending up in Carshalton via Wallington, both in the London Borough of Sutton, I always considered myself a South - NOT Sarf - Londoner!)

About twelve years ago I came across the David Lean directed and Noel Coward penned 1944 film *'This Happy Breed,'* a story about the Gibbons family living in Earlsfield between the two world wars. Most of the main characters shared the names of my parents, aunts and uncles; even the cat was called Percy - my dad's middle name - this kind of freaked me out a little!

As for my mum's family, her two sisters and parents all decided to seek a new life in America before I was born - Mum stayed to marry my dad. Sister Marje hooked up with Edwin, an ex-US serviceman ('overpaid, oversexed and over here' as they used to say), so I think that was the driving force behind the move - sister Bettie had already married Les and went too. There was another 'secret' sister who was never referred to; all I knew was that she had what we now would call 'mental health issues', but in those days, things were handled somewhat differently and such people were often sent to a 'home'. I remember being taken by Mum to visit her in Clapham when I was about seven or eight and sworn to secrecy about it. To this day I know nothing more, although I have a hunch it may have been as simple as having a child out of wedlock.

I never knew my maternal grandfather, and only met my grandmother on the one occasion she came to the UK. My grandfather had been a gardener when he lived in England and loved the outside life, which for someone moving to Phoenix, Arizona, isn't a great occupation - he died of skin cancer. Shortly before I was born, Mum travelled to the USA to visit the family. Back in the mid-fifties air travel was hugely expensive so she travelled alone on the Queen Mary and then by train to Phoenix. I discovered many years later that while she was there her brother-in-law, Edwin, tried to rape her. This was common knowledge amongst the family, and over the years my parents visited Edwin, Marje, Les and Bettie in the US. They all came over to the UK reasonably often, and they continued to get on with each other. The incident was swept under the carpet as these things were in those days. Talk about skeletons in closets - different times eh? Or maybe not, as it sounds like the sort of thing you hear on *The Jeremy Kyle Show* or see on *EastEnders*.

Dad bought a second-hand Morris Oxford the day I was born, to bring me home from the hospital. I think it might have been my parents' first car and like many people, they'd previously got around on motorbikes. Dad competed in motorcycle trials, and Mum got into trouble with the neighbours for riding the family 'outfit' (motorcycle and side-car), up and down Muchelney Road on two wheels. If you'd known her in later years that would have been hard to imagine.

Dad had served on US aircraft carriers in the merchant service during WW2. He was a pacifist, and didn't want to be put in the position of actually shooting someone, and thought he'd be better off in a protected trade rather than being called up - or being imprisoned as a conscientious objector. The long and short of that though, meant that he ended up being fired upon at sea, dive-bombed by Kamikaze planes, sunk twice and rescued, and very nearly blown up. He rarely spoke of his wartime experiences, but I do wish I'd asked more questions while he was alive, I can't imagine the horrors he must have seen and been through. His love of boats, water, and the sea in general always remained to the day he died.

Having trained as a tool-maker, my old man was an excellent engineer, and while we were living in St. Helier, he was in business with his two younger brothers Jack and Frank, with their own light engineering company 'Gibbons Brothers'. Older brother John was an engineer too, and ran his own company.

My parents had aspirations to move out of social housing as soon as possible - Dad disliked what he felt was 'subsidised living' - and so that was to be. The firm was doing well, and to keep the Morris Oxford company, he'd bought a 1937 Rolls-Royce. This sounds very grand, but at the time it was a twenty-two-year-old 'banger', and it became a habit of his to give the appearance of doing rather better than he actually was - a habit I fear I have also taken to! But still, it was a Rolls, and the locals took a dislike to it, stubbing out cigarettes and spitting on it. But to be fair, this was on a council estate when most people didn't even have a car. Once, when Dad was asked why we were moving from the estate, he replied, 'Because we need a bigger house - the butler keeps stubbing his toe on the wine rack!'

This gave Dad the motivation to move on, and in 1960 we moved to Wallington, Surrey. 63 Ross Road was a delightful semi-detached house amongst a row of many similar houses common in the surrounding areas. It had a good amount of space to the side on which Dad built himself a double garage-cum-workshop, and when I say built himself, I do mean that he did it all on his own, from footings to roof.

While living on the St. Helier Estate, my parents got involved with the local church - St. Peter's C of E in Bishopsford Road, just along from my nan's house. I'm not sure what motivated them to join St. Peter's as neither of them ever struck me as terribly religious, but involved they were. Attached to the church was a parish youth club - The Crosskeys, which had been opened by the Queen Mum and rising rock 'n' roll star Adam Faith, and this is where their involvement chiefly lay - in running the club and the associated amateur dramatic group. As a small child, I spent quite a lot of my time with them there, and when we moved to Wallington they continued their support of the club.

In keeping the youth of the estate off the streets, my parents became friendly with many of the club's members, some of whom I'm pleased to say remain friends of mine to this day. My dad was no fool, and realised that this group of young people constituted a

8

potential workforce, and when he hatched a plan to install a swimming pool at Ross Road, this became useful.

Now at the time in the early 60s, domestic swimming pools were not common, and reserved for the rich. Dad was not rich, but once he set his mind to something it would usually happen. After all, it was only a hole in the ground full of water…!

He did his research, and with some help from the structural engineers at SGB, a company Gibbons Brothers worked with, favours were done, and a plan was formulated - all he needed to do was dig the hole. Enter the youth club workforce!

So that there would be no waste to dispose of, the pool was to be 'half in-half out' whereby the surplus soil dug was relocated at the perimeter of the hole creating the 'walls'. The hoard of youth club members would come around at weekends, and using nothing but shovels, picks, wheelbarrows and hard graft, dug the hole, fuelled by roast dinner cooked by Mum and cans of Long Life or Party Seven beer. SGB loaned the shuttering to form the walls - I suspect a backhander was involved - and with a further backhander to a driver of a cement mixer lorry, the concrete was delivered one Sunday and the youth club team wheelbarrowed it all in from the road outside.

The upshot of this was that those who dug the hole pretty much had open access to the pool once it was done. On many summer Sundays they would turn up unannounced and make use of the 'facilities' while Mum would stretch out roast lunch for three to five, six, seven or more. I'd be sent down the road to the corner off-licence to pick up Party Sevens (large cans holding seven pints of cheap beer), or tins of Long Life. Sure, I wasn't old enough to buy beer, but Dad had an 'arrangement' with the owner of the 'offie' who turned a blind eye. Dad was the sort of person who could have an 'arrangement' with pretty much anyone!

So our Ross Road house appeared to be the home of a wealthy family, what with its swimming pool, a large garage, a Rolls in the drive – and later an American Chevrolet Impala, and Dad had also now begun to race inshore hydroplane boats - it all appeared very grand. Wealth had nothing to do with it, it was all hard work, canny buying, and the benefit of friends who were keen to help.

*   *   *

Now I don't ever recall expressing a desire to own a dog, but when I was about ten or eleven years old Dad came home with a pedigree Old English Sheepdog, by the name of 'Bowser-Smythe the Third'. Daft as a brush it was – as they all are, and it was of course my task to take it for walks. With hair over its eyes hindering its view Bowser would regularly walk straight into a tree, shake his head and continue on his way.

One day in the winter, while I was at school with snow on the ground, Mum let the dog into the garden to 'make himself comfortable'. Bowser trotted around the perimeter of the pool, stopped suddenly, slipped on the snow, and went in headfirst.

The pool had been drained for the winter, but by now it had about a foot of stagnant rainwater in its bottom – covered in ice, and Bowser was decidedly unhappy about being in there - Mum was even less happy in having no choice but to get in there with him, and hoist the sodden and panicking dog up out of the pool. I arrived home from school to find a tearful and somewhat distressed mother drying Bowser with a hair dryer after giving him a bath.

A few days later Bowser had gone. No, he hadn't succumbed to the ordeal, Mum had decided he was 'A bloody liability!' so he was sold. That six months was the sum total of my pet ownership.

*   *   *

We stayed in Ross Road until 1974, when property developers descended on the row of houses of which number 63 was one. All the neighbours were happy to take the quick buck, but Dad was happy there, and knew that without our house, the development couldn't go ahead - so he stuck out for more money. To say that this caused friction between ourselves and the eager neighbours is an understatement, but Dad stuck to his guns and got a far better deal that the others.

So, we needed to find a new home within a couple of months. I don't recall my parents looking at any houses at all, and I'm not sure how Dad actually discovered that the house that was to be our new home was for sale - and it wasn't far away in West Street, Carshalton. Number 12, 'The Yews' had been owned by a recently deceased eccentric recluse by the name of Bob Pratt, He didn't live in it himself, but had lived in a terraced house across the road. And the estate was being sold by his brother Albert, who was equally as eccentric and was living in an old Triumph Spitfire in the driveway of The Yews.

'The Yews' in West Street shortly after we bought it and just before we moved in

It was a rather grand but dilapidated-looking timber clad building with a concrete wall built like a fortress around the front garden. And here's the kicker; Dad bought it while Mum was away in Phoenix, Arizona, visiting her family. He drove past it on the way back from collecting Mum from Heathrow airport and declared, 'That's the house we've bought!'

Now it would have been nice to have viewed the inside of the house, only there was a difficulty - every room was filled to the ceiling with junk. Old furniture, boxes of bulk purchased items, old and new clothes - everything and anything you could imagine. In some rooms you could barely open the door to enter. The cellar was full to the brim with coal, and the garden (where it wasn't overgrown), was home to old machinery and car parts.

There was a large garage to the rear - equally full of old stuff, and a lean-to garage to the side of the house - again full. There was also a two-storey brick built 'Coach-house' - also full. And Dad bought it lock, stock, and barrel. All of this junk was now ours. It became apparent that old Bob Pratt had been ingratiating himself to widowed old ladies (several at a time), becoming the beneficiary in their wills, and 'storing' all the inherited and unwanted junk. Except, not all of it was junk, there were a couple of vintage cars in there which we kept and began (but never finished) restorations on.

Was Bob knocking the old dears off? We'll never know, but he accrued a large amount of 'stock' in a very short time…

*   *   *

At the time Dad employed a chap called Bob Hudson on a casual basis to help at G.B. Tools - the hire shop he now owned and where I worked (the letters G.B. stood for Gibbons Brothers – not Great Britain, although we had more than one rep come into the shop asking to speak with Mr. Tools). Bob always believed there to be a 'pot of gold' hidden among this pile of old rubbish, and he helped my dad clear the house while I looked after and ran the hire shop.

Dad found someone to buy the several tons of coal (which he and Bob shovelled up from the cellar), and while clearing up Bob came across a box, a bit like a treasure chest, high up on the window ledge. 'This is it!' he exclaimed, 'I've found it!' and lifted the box down from the window sill. As he did so, the old box gave way at its bottom, depositing the dusty contents all over Bob. Bob looked at the lid of the box, and began to read, 'In loving memory….' It's fair to say that he cleared the stairs in about three paces, and drove home at the speed of light to have a shower and wash his clothes.

No 'pot of gold' was ever found, but there were some rather nice things - some of which I still own, such as a pleasant Grandfather clock, a three-hundred-year-old coffer, a splendid large pine

Welsh dresser, and a beautiful antique diamond ring. As for everything else, anything of value was sold. If it could be burned, it went on the bonfire (which I believe burned continuously for more than three weeks!), and the rest went in many, many skips.

The house we'd just moved out of

(There were many boxes of old photographs, and in one we discovered a picture of a house that looked familiar, a house into which a 'plane had crashed into its roof. It was in fact a photograph of 63 Ross Road, the very house out of which we'd just moved! Not only was this spookily coincidental, it explained why there had been newer beams fitted, and evidence of repairs in the loft. Further investigation found that being not far from both Croydon and Kenley Airports, two RAF 'planes had been engaged in battle practice overhead and hit one another, with one 'plane crashing in flames into the roof of number 63, and the other landing in Tharp Road, a short distance away, but only after its fuel tank had become detached and fallen through the roof of another nearby house. Both pilots escaped by means of their parachutes).

The perimeter wall at the front got knocked down and an 'in & out' driveway created, and once the house was empty enough, we moved into what was in fact, a pretty much derelict building, which gradually got restored and decorated and became a rather splendid five-bedroom family home. Although, being old and timber-clad it was cold and always in need of a coat of paint.

The garages were useful and my dad and I spent a lot of time playing with cars. A swimming pool was installed, again on a budget (and with previous experience - a simpler design), but this time rather than employ the shovels of thirsty volunteers, Dad brought in an excavator. And in spite of not having central heating upstairs (on more than one occasion there was ice on the *inside* of my bedroom window), it was a lovely, happy home.

I lived in West Street with my parents until 1985, when an opportunity to work for a professional Top Fuel drag race team in America came up. With massive help from Dad I'd now built and raced three drag race cars, and I had decided to stop racing after Easter 1984. My race car had been sold, I'd built and sold a beach buggy, and I now possessed the funds to be able to buy a 1978 Chevrolet Corvette as my daily driver - age 27. I'd also continued an interest in drag racing, helping out other racers - in particular Tony Morris who bought my race car and took it to Germany - we remain great friends to this day. I'd continued to read the American weekly paper '*National Dragster*', and answered a 'Staff Wanted' advert spotted within. The only thing is - I told no one what I'd done; not Dad, Mum, or Paula, the girlfriend with whom I was in a pretty committed relationship at the time. And then I got a letter saying the job was mine if I wanted it!

To say that it came as a surprise to all of them - not least myself is an understatement! But for me, selfishly, it was a chance of a lifetime. So a week later I packed my bags and was on my way to live in Columbus, Ohio, not knowing when I might return.

I'll come back to that.

2

Approaching madness

I was at 1a Railway Approach pretty much on a daily basis, and as you might glean from the name, Wallington railway station was at the top of this short road.

Dad started the hire shop about when I started secondary school, and I used to go with him in the morning, help open up the shop, and then catch the train to school - Glastonbury's Boys School on the St. Helier Estate. I'd come back in the afternoon and help in the shop until closing time when Dad would drive the short distance home to Ross Road. I also helped in the shop on Saturdays, but we ended up making that our early closing day when we realised that anyone who wanted to hire something for just a day would have to pay for the whole weekend!

Proud Dad outside GB Tools Plant Hire in Railway Approach Wallington

Next door to our G.B. Tools Hire Shop was The Saladin Cafe. We rented the yard attached to the cafe for the hire shop, and when The Saladin came up for sale, we were going to lose the use of the yard, so Dad had little choice but to buy the cafe in order to keep trading. How my Mum felt about being made to run a cafe I will never know! We rented out the rooms above as a flat and offices to various people, and there was a tiny cab office on the ground floor. It all sounds very grand, but frankly it was a poorly maintained and grubby little dive.

To the other side of the hire shop was an automotive electrical specialist, and beyond that a small kiosk type shop which changed use on a regular basis. Just across the main road was Melbourne Road which had on opposite corners the International Stores and The Melbourne pub.

Behind the row of shops in the approach was a scrap metal and vehicle breakers yard, owned and run by a character called 'Curley' Day (I'm not sure I ever knew his real first name), located in the area adjacent to Wallington Station car park, known as Forsdick's Yard. It was located up an alleyway between The Saladin and a furniture shop in Manor Road, Wallington. Along with the breakers yard there was an abundance of lock-ups where car mechanics and panel beaters plied their trade – every one of them a 'character'. It was a complete den of iniquity, and the police were frequent visitors. At one time Curley's breakers yard didn't have a guard dog but a guard bear… I kid you not!!

In my teens, I earned pocket money there helping out several of the traders – at fourteen I was already spraying cars. I also helped dismantle some of the 'old bangers' in the yard - I remember an Allard and a Singer, and helped cut the back off of a Humber Pullman so that a Harvey Frost crane could be fitted. It was quite a common occurrence to hear a loud explosion when Gerry 'Guppy' Upton would blow up a petrol tank while using his 'gas axe'. How we laughed! I recall separating lead sheathed copper cables and melting the lead into ingots along with other sheet lead. It was many years later, I realised it was stolen goods (some of it probably from the railway lines next door), and I was hiding the evidence. I imagine the lead fumes weren't doing me any good either…

Tool hire shops were uncommon in those days, and Dad spotted an opportunity where it might be profitable to open one. The next nearest hire shop was a company called 'The Ladder Hire Company' some distance away in Beckenham, and they primarily hired out, you guessed it, ladders. Having started the shop on the back of Gibbons Brothers Engineering with brothers Jack and

16

Frank, the brothers decided that dealing with the public wasn't for them and it wasn't bringing in the hoped-for income. Calling it 'sweet shop stuff money', the two businesses amicably separated.

At this time Dad was still an undiagnosed dyslexic, which probably accounts for why the business was not the success it could have been. But Dad was a 'dealer', and the hire shop brought in a wide range of people who liked 'a deal'.

(If you're familiar with the 80s TV programme *Minder*, you'll be aware of a character called Arthur Daley, a trader who flew under the radar - never a crook, but often onto the end of something 'a bit dodgy'. Well Dad was a bit like that. Not in the 'trilby titfer and camel coat' kind of way, but always with 'a wad' of cash in his pocket, and he could be relied on to be ready for a deal. And the sort of customers who used a hire shop were the sort of people who always had something to move on - often quickly).

I left school in the summer of 1972 aged fifteen - and that was the last year kids were able to do so. It was always assumed I'd go and work with Dad, and frankly he needed the help - read 'cheap labour' - and I've often said that I got a better education in the way of life in that hire shop than I ever would at school.

The primary clientele of G. B. Tools hire shop were local builders, roofers, decorators and mechanics - usually small firms who used us for equipment they didn't have already. We stocked small tools such as Kango hammers, drills, cement mixers, lawn-mowers, ladders, trestles, engine hoists and jacks, and this was in the days before credit cards, so anyone hiring an item was asked to leave a deposit and show a proof of identity. Generally, the deposit would be nowhere near the value of the item - not even second-hand, so we were often taking a bit of a risk as to whether the tool might (or might not), be returned. The only proof of identity was usually a driving licence, and this was before they included photographs.

This element of risk meant that I had to become a very good judge of character before hiring out something to someone for the first, or even subsequent, times. There were some expensive errors during the learning curve, but I got a keen eye on who was 'right' and who might be a 'wrong-un'. This is a skill I believe I carry with me to this day, and I quickly know who to trust.

Some customers would always try to barter you down in price, and when returning the tool, would often say that it didn't work properly and demand a discount or a refund. It was not unusual to see that they had clearly done something to the equipment on purpose (disconnect a wire or even swap the earth and live)! Others would nearly always plead poverty, even when their address indicated that they lived in an affluent area, and would often return equipment late but still only want to pay the initial hire period.

We would occasionally have to go on 'snatchbacks' to recover equipment not returned. Knocking on doors in the evenings to collect what was rightfully yours rarely went down well with people. Sometimes it was a house on which our customer had been working and they would have no idea the equipment was on hire. Only once did I see my dad lose control when he knocked on a door to ask for a pair of axle stands back, only to be told to 'Piss off'. Dad came back to the truck, grabbed a sledgehammer from the back and started back to the house. I grabbed his arm and told him to 'Leave it - it's only a pair of axle stands!' and fortunately he did, but he was trembling with rage. I'm not sure I'd ever seen that in him before or since. A few days later the man returned the axle stands.

It was routine for many of our regulars to come in first thing in the morning to collect what they needed and return in the evening, and it didn't hurt that The Melbourne pub was just over the road. In those days there were strict licensing hours, with pubs not opening until 5.30pm. So just as we closed, almost on a daily basis there would be a group of rough looking builders standing in, or in the better weather, outside the shop waiting for the pub to open. If they really couldn't wait they'd pre-load on cheap beer from the off-licence a few yards away.

This time of day also coincided with the train offloading its cargo of commuters, who had to pass this rowdy rabble on their way home. For the rowdy rabble regularly standing outside our shop this had the added bonus of them being able to eye up the 'crumpet' as they tottered down the approach, and totter they usually did as it was almost unthinkable for women to be seen in 'flats' in those days. Yes, lewd comments were made - and ignored. I can't imagine how these ladies must have felt having to put up with this abuse almost on a daily basis. Many would choose to walk down the opposite side of the street in an attempt to avoid it, but this only resulted in increased volume. I don't think it would happen today - different times...

To say that the people I was mixing with, not just our regulars, but the characters from Forsdick's Yard round the back were 'colourful', would be an understatement. That said, I was 'Reg's boy' and they looked after me. Yes, all of them were scoundrels, some were petty crooks too. Stolen 'gear' was common, I also saw guns and heard of their use on occasion. The police would sometimes come by to see if we'd seen a particular 'face' lately. And yes, Dad would buy a bit of 'hooky gear' occasionally - I can't condone it, I'm not proud of it, but it was normal at the time. On more than one occasion we were offered our own equipment back!

One time, a couple of these cut-price villains stole the contents of the back of a lorry thinking that it was booze – but it was trainers! They off-loaded them pair by pair to anyone and everyone they knew - including me, telling everyone to be a bit careful about when and where they wore them so as not to arouse suspicion. They were black Gola running shoes with luminous yellow stripes down either side, and one evening I walked into The Melbourne and was almost blinded by row upon row of gleaming new trainers! Low profile this was not - and just for the record, I wasn't wearing mine.[1]

The death knell of the Approach sounded when one night there was a fire in Forsdick's Yard - and not a small fire either. We were alerted to this and made our way to see what was going on,

---

[1] *This event is very similar to a storyline in Minder, when Arthur Daley was knocking out 'exclusive' (stolen) sport coats, and everyone in The Windsor Club was wearing one.*

and clearly the Fire Brigade were concerned it could spread to the shops in front.

Even from the entrance to the Approach you could see it was an impressive blaze. Car fuel tanks were exploding, as were gas cylinders (the acetylene ones were particularly spectacular - a piece of one was later discovered in the car park of The Melbourne pub over the road), and debris was falling into the surrounding streets. What was also concerning was that we kept a couple of cars in the station car park (thanks to a back-hander to the station manager), directly adjacent to the Forsdick's Yard. Fortunately the brigade managed to push them to safety, but not before the fibreglass bonnet of an MG Midget suffered burns.

Of course, no-one will ever know the truth, possibly it was an insurance job, or more likely it was the owner of the land wanted everyone off and this was an easy way to 'repossess' the property. None of the businesses recovered and the land was subsequently sold for development - suspiciously quickly. Not one person I knew believed the fire was an accident.

It wasn't too long before all the shops in Railway Approach came under offer. Dad, as usual, negotiated a really good deal, and we moved to a corner shop a mile and a quarter away in Hackbridge. What was once the Saladin Dad had rented out to American Autoparts who then relocated to Thornton Heath, so that was the end of an era.

Railway Approach and Forsdick's Yard was completely re-developed, the station got a make-over and a new car park, offices were built. A bus stand now exists on top of what was once G.B. Tools Plant Hire, and the Royal Mail sorting office now occupies the space once known as Forsdick's Yard.

3

Ah, that explains a lot

Before I was born Dad and his brothers - all of them engineers - had an interest in motorcycles; well to be honest, cars at the time were an unaffordable luxury. And back then, if you owned a motorbike or car you learned how to keep it running and on the road.

Dad climbing up onto brother Jack's shoulder 1948ish

After WW2 in the second half of the 1940s, and after my father was released from the Merchant Navy, he would occasionally race his motorcycle – yes, the one he was riding to work and back every day. This was primarily trials events at Brands Hatch on grass - before the track proper was laid. He would ride to Brands, race, and ride back home again.

When he and my mum moved to Bishopsford Road on the St. Helier Estate, motorcycles were their only form of transport, and they bought an 'outfit', or motorcycle and sidecar. As mentioned earlier, when I arrived they got sensible and bought a second-hand Morris Oxford, which was joined by the first Rolls-Royce - a 1937 Park Ward Sport Saloon. I have a memory of being flung from the rear seat when Dad braked hard, and banging my head on the winder for the glass central division - I still have the scar!

Going hydroplane racing could be a simple affair in the 1960s -
Outside 63 Ross Road circa 1965

Soon after we moved to Ross Road in Wallington, Dad discovered hydroplane racing. I don't know how this came about, but eventually all four brothers competed and pretty much dominated the scene in the 1960s. For the uninitiated, hydroplanes are little more than a plank of wood, not much bigger than an ironing board, powered by a powerful (in this case), two-stroke motor. Dad exclusively used the German made twin-cylinder König 350cc motor (later he became good friends with the designer and manufacturer Dieter König), which was specifically designed for the purpose. There was also a 500cc version which was a four-cylinder 'boxer' motor - much like a VW. I used to have the run of the lakes wearing a life-jacket bearing the slogan 'The König Kid' on the back. This all meant that I spent a large part of my childhood weekends at a gravel pit near Feltham in Middlesex, which had been filled with water and now formed Bedfont Lake where motorboat racing and water skiing took place.

Dad was particularly competitive, making the most of every skill he possessed to squeeze as much performance as possible out of the 350cc two-stroke engines on a budget. (This was a talent I tried to emulate and later use in my own motorsport activities).

He was an early adopter of 'marginal gains', employing tricks like polishing the underside of his craft to make it more readily slip over the water. Often his boat would beat those with a larger 500cc capacity. This gave him great satisfaction.

Most of the two-stroke engines ran on a fuel known as 'dope' which was methanol mixed with Castrol R (which had a very distinct smell in use). Two-stroke engines are notoriously hard to start when cold - even more so when using methanol, and the start process involved wrapping a rope around the flywheel on top of the motor and tugging it hard. It could be a lengthy and frustrating procedure - once warm, it was much easier. So my dad used to 'psyche' his fellow racers out. He would pull into a layby not far from the lake, getting the motor started and warming it up, which meant that when he got to the lake and the boat was in the water, the engine was already warm and it would start first pull, while his contemporaries continued to tug on their ropes. I'm not sure anyone ever cottoned on to what he was doing.

He did well, becoming British champion, and in 1965 was invited along with his brother Jack to race at the European championships on Tegeler See in Berlin. It must be remembered that at this time Germany was divided, and the Berlin Wall was up. The Second World War remained fresh in people's memories, and driving to Berlin with two boats on a trailer was a huge undertaking. Most people didn't even have a telephone. At the time there were strict limits on how much cash you could take with you, and all the contents of the car and trailer - including tools and spares - had to be listed on a 'carnet' to be stamped by the customs authorities at each border. On the return, if the vehicle was inspected and anything was missing - or added - it had to be accounted for. And of course, the East/West border needed to be crossed.

Leaving me and Mum at home, with his brother Jack and a map of the continent in hand, he left to represent the UK in 350cc hydroplane racing. We heard nothing until he returned nearly a week later.

Dad cutting in front of brother Jack at Bedfont

I can't recall how they did, but Dad made some good friends and returned in 1966, this time to West Germany, to Baldeneysee near Essen. The journey was shorter and at least they didn't have to tackle the Berlin Wall, but it was still a fair undertaking, again leaving Mum and me at home. To our surprise, he returned with two boats on the trailer - one on top of the other. While there, he'd bought a 'prone' hydroplane, one in which you lay flat on your stomach rather than kneel. These were becoming common in Europe, but this was the first example in the UK. Quite how he managed to pay for it with the limited funds allowed to be taken out of the country I don't know, and to top that, in spite of the carnet regulations, he'd managed to sneak it back without anyone questioning it. Basically, he'd just smuggled a whole hydroplane into the country!

The hydroplane Dad smuggled in from Germany. Note his 'state of the art' invention of the use of a bucket to prevent the carburettor from ingesting water

24

Two years later he returned to Essen, this time taking me and Mum and a couple of friends - we'd make it more of a holiday this time. We stayed in dormitories in the clubhouse by the lake, and the bedding consisted of a strange thing called a 'duvet'... Having never seen one before we weren't sure whether you were supposed to get inside it or not.

Mum, Dad, and me enjoying breakfast outside our dormitory at Baldeneysee in Essen

At the reception in the clubhouse the night before all the drivers were presented and their respective national anthems played. Naturally half the room stood up when it was Germany's turn, quite a few from Holland, and then it came to Great Britain. The three of us stood up - feeling more than a little self-conscious.

Again, sadly I have no record of how well it went, but I do remember the strange custom of having a slice of lemon in Coca-Cola, mayonnaise on chips, and being bought a proper pair of traditional 'lederhosen', which being eleven years old, I was happy to wear *all* the time.

(For my fiftieth birthday, Alli paid for me to have a 'hydroplane experience day'. Leaving Alli's sister to babysit Scott, we went to a lake in Bristol - one that I instantly recognised as somewhere my dad used to race. While the boats we used were the same as those that he used to race, for safety reasons the motors weren't quite as powerful. It was a complete blast, and it made me realise that my old man must have had balls the size of coconuts to race these things at speed.

The day also allowed for piloting a Formula 2 style hydroplane, a boat in which you were seated more like you would be in a car, rather than the prone position of a conventional hydro. They were more powerful, but not much faster as they were bigger, but the cornering forces were immense - far greater than those I'd experienced in any of my race cars. Of course I loved it, and it was a real joy to be able to experience what my dad used to – if only just a little bit).

Dad's racing reputation had grown during this time, and when it came to needing someone to carry out a hydroplane 'stunt' for a Timex watch commercial, Dad was the man. The stunt involved fixing a Timex Marlin watch to the centre of the boat's propeller, driving that boat around a lake, and then taking the boat over a ski ramp. Of course, Dad was approached and he said 'yes' immediately, and once again I doubt that my mother had much to say about it, but the fact that he was to be paid £350 (approximately £5,350 in today's money), for the job, may have had something to do with it! They would have been able to pay off the mortgage and have some left over. To put things in perspective, the price of our house when they bought it in 1961, was £3,000.

No one had driven a hydroplane over a ski ramp before, so there was no idea whether it could be done - or not. Dad had visions of powering up the ramp only to have the craft disintegrate around him, leaving him flying through the air, cartoon- style, in the position of 'driving a hydroplane'.

An old hydroplane was procured and strengthened, 'skids' were attached to the bottom for less surface friction, a grab rail around the steering wheel fitted so he could 'lock' the steering in position with his grip, and a less temperamental Mercury outboard motor fitted in place of the highly strung König racing engine. Using Dad's engineering skills, a fitting to take the watch was manufactured and held onto the centre of the propeller by the prop nut. The motor was fitted in such a way that it would 'kick out' when the underwater unit hit the ramp, and return by the use of bungee cords aided by application of the throttle to drive the motor back into the boat.

Testing the jumping hydroplane at Bedfont

The film crew came to the house to carry out tests, and being in the fortunate position of having a swimming pool, the hydroplane was lifted into the pool, tethered and fired up, complete with the Timex watch beneath the water - everything survived.

Dad also constructed a shorter than normal ski ramp as it wasn't certain he could achieve the necessary speed for the boat to make it over the top of a regular one, and to help, before the jump it was to be smothered in grease. The hydro was painted in bright orange so it would show up better on the black and white TV images, and (rather cheekily), 'Gibbons Brothers Engineering' attached to the flanks using waterslide transfers.

Again, again, again!

Dad, with brothers Jack and Frank as crew, left for Coniston Water in the Lake District - the very place that Sir Donald Campbell had died earlier that year, attempting to break the water speed record. They were gone for a week, and again, Mum and I were left at home. At least this time she got the occasional telephone call while they were away. I often wondered how she felt about having my father disappear on 'adventures' without her, but I guess that they had both lived through World War II, and that was something people simply got used to. I'm not sure I was old enough to appreciate the gravity of these things.

Actor John Bentley about to deliver his piece to camera

I know from personal experience, that filming is a frustrating and time-consuming business. Of course, Dad was apprehensive and the delays

28

didn't help. He'd go out and circle the lake and the ramp to prepare to jump for the first time, only for the shot to be called off at the last second for technical reasons. Finally, with all the preparations made to the best of their abilities, he approached the ramp at full chat, clenched his buttocks, shut down the throttle so as not to over-rev the motor, locked his hand around the steering and grab-rail. Bang, he hit the ramp, a second later he and the boat were flying through the air, opening the throttle to drive the boat out of the 'hole' created by landing in the water. Success! Everything had worked exactly as it should.

Now he had to 'beach' the boat so that the camera could zoom in on the watch to show it was still ticking as it should. The director made a mark on the beach to show where he wanted Dad to stop. Dad said 'Mate, I've never done this before, I could end up in those fucking trees!'

'I could end up in those fucking trees!'

Again, after the first attempt he worked it out and could adjust his speed accordingly (without, by the way, any way of knowing what that speed was). Actor John Bentley - famous for being on *Crossroads* - was there with microphone in hand, carrying out the following dialogue, '*Timex watches take a licking and still keep ticking'*, as the camera zoomed in on the sodden but still functioning watch. Of course, the film crew wanted more takes, and Dad made more and more jumps over the ramp. Having got the first one out of the way he was quite enjoying himself and didn't really want to stop.

Dad and his brothers were treated like royalty, and everything had gone according to plan. Once back in Wallington his fame grew to having photos of himself and pictures of the jumping boat on the wall of Fishers' hairdresser.

I still have the watch - and it still works.

The new Timex Marlin, and the original used in the 'Torture test'!

(In 2018, due to the renewed popularity of 'beater' watches, Timex re-introduced The Marlin. I wrote to them with the story of my dad and the jump – hoping they might service the original watch for me. They didn't, but sent me a brand-new Marlin watch instead – but I'd still like to get the original one serviced!!)

When a visitor came to our home a short while ago, they saw the display of photos of my dad racing in his hydroplane and flying through the air off the ramp. 'Ah, that explains a lot,' he said, referring to my own motorsport activities.

There was a further TV commercial that the brothers were involved in, this time for Ajax pan scourers. My uncle John was the pilot assisted by my dad, and a friend from the Crosskeys Youth Club, Fred Yule. A pan scourer was attached to the underwater unit of the motor, driven at speed around the lake, and then the scourer was shown to have plenty of 'suds' left in it. A pan made dirty for the purpose of demonstration was then cleaned. I think Dad let John do this one as it wasn't nearly dangerous enough for him!

At the end of 1968, the brothers came to the realization that their successful engineering business was suffering, as they were spending a lot of time racing and not enough time working on the business. Dad stopped racing 'cold turkey' and sold everything, and never went to a racing lake or watched a race again – I think he knew he wouldn't be able to resist.

And then a year later when I was twelve, something else took its place.

4

It was inevitable and unavoidable

Just across the road from the shop was The Melbourne pub. One of the staff who lived above the pub had dabbled with kart racing, and for whatever reason, decided it wasn't for him. So, we ended up with a kart. It was a Zip Californian powered by a BM100JB 100cc single-cylinder two-stroke engine. We'd never even been to a kart track (you'll discover that this sort of thing happened a lot), so one Saturday we drove to our local track in Surbiton to check things out. There, in the middle of suburban Surrey, was a track which surrounded a football pitch. There was a clubhouse and playground too. I was immediately struck by the Ford Model T hot rod in the car park belonging to guitarist Jeff Beck. He too had just gone there for the day out (right there and then I decided that one day I'd own a Model T hot rod). Jeff lived in Demesne Road just around the corner from us in Ross Road, Wallington, and subsequently I'd see him tooling around the local streets. I never got to meet him though.

(Some members of a band shared a flat a little further up Ross Road. The locals said it was The Small Faces, but with one of them apparently being Ronnie Wood, The Jeff Beck Group would make more sense - with Beck living just around the corner! When I was twelve or thirteen – at the time a Scout, and as it was 'Bob A Job Week' - I knocked on the door. The door was opened by a 'rock 'n roll' looking bloke with a substantial 'roll-up' in his hand onto a smoke-filled hallway. It turned out they had no jobs that needed doing, but he pushed some loose change into my hand anyway and closed to door. Was it Ronnie? Or even Rod Stewart? I doubt I'll ever know).[2]

---

[2] *'Bob A Job Week' was an annual charity event which raised funds for the Scout movement. Teenage Scouts would roam the streets dressed in uniform not unlike that of a military youth army, knocking on the doors of perfect strangers, and offering to carry out menial jobs in return for no less than a shilling (a 'bob'), whereupon they would be invited into these*

Having checked the lay of the land, we discovered that I could drive the very same kart as a 'junior' (up to sixteen years of age), that Dad could race as a senior. I was equipped with what was needed, helmet, protective PVC overalls, and an RAC licence and set off for some practice. I took to it quite quickly, and so did Dad, but because the karts were direct drive and needed to be 'bump started', it was an issue for him, as I wasn't man enough to start the kart for him. The technique was to lift the rear of the machine off the ground, run a few paces, drop the kart to the ground to get the engine turning over, and then pushing for as long as it took to fire the damn thing up, and as mentioned earlier, two-stroke motors aren't the easiest of things to start. I wasn't strong enough to do that at age twelve. So clearly, I got more time in the seat than Dad.

Having now successfully made the kart mine by default, I started racing on a casual basis. The trouble was, I wasn't very good. I got one third place trophy, but even then, we'd had to argue with the time keepers about the number of laps I'd completed.

Dad stripped the kart engine down and applied his extensive two-stroke knowledge to get the best out of the diminutive little motor. This only served to highlight my poor racing skills when we lent our kart to a fellow senior racer who went on to dominate the event - offering to buy the machine at the end of the day. Needless to say, we didn't sell and carried on until I was sixteen.

The experience taught me a great deal of early lessons in preparing a racing machine. Of course, I was shown how to service and maintain it, mix the fuel and so on, and Dad would sometimes 'test' me by deliberately putting a minor fault on the kart, a loose bolt or crimped fuel line and so on, to see if I picked up on it during service - and sometimes I didn't. I also learnt that if something broke, you don't simply repair it, you discover the cause and repair it in a way that it will never break again. I am now meticulous in my preparation of racing machines.

---

homes to carry out any task required of them without complaint. These days it's hard to imagine that such a thing was ever allowed to happen!

*   *   *

We hadn't at first appreciated that living and working in Wallington, we inadvertently found ourselves in the middle of a UK drag racing hot spot.

Dad and I were already aware of drag racing as he used to buy the American magazine *Hot Rod*, partly for the cars, but mainly because at the time they used to run a monthly feature on power boat racing. So, I was already cognizant of vehicles like Jeff Beck's 'Boston Strangler' hot rod seen at Surbiton kart track, and Dad was already friendly with Tony Densham at Sutton Rebore. Tony was a pioneer of British drag racing, along with his partners Harry Worrell and Peter Billinton. Dad had been using their machine shop services since he'd been riding trials bikes.

One day I noticed a dragster in the window of a tyre repair shop in Stafford Road - two streets along and parallel to our Ross Road. Until now I'd only seen pictures of dragsters having read Dad's *Hot Rod* mags, and possessed a signed photograph of Tony Densham in his car 'Commuter'. I told Dad about the dragster and we both popped along to see what was what.

We introduced ourselves to Denis Acott and Dave Prior who were the managers of Tyresales, they showed us around the Jaguar-powered 'Helkat' dragster and told us what they could about drag racing. Dad expressed an interest in perhaps having a go himself at it sometime, and thought nothing more about it.

A few weeks later we took a tyre there to be repaired, and were told of a dragster rolling chassis for sale that they knew of. Dad bought it sight unseen for £110 and sent me and John Eve – a fella who occasionally helped out in the hire shop - to collect it from Sudbury in Suffolk in our truck. A Daimler engine from a 250 saloon was procured from 'Curley' Day's breakers' yard behind the shop, as was a Ford Thames van three-speed gearbox. The kart had already been sold, I was sixteen, we had the makings of a dragster - and yet we'd never been to a drag strip. Sound familiar?

We made our first trip to Santa Pod Raceway in 1973 and were blown away by what we saw. Such a wide range of exotic - and not so exotic - machinery, with nearly everything having been hand-made and designed by each vehicle owner - this clearly appealed to the engineer in my father.

*   *   *

During these early days, we also discovered that in the next street along, in Melbourne Road, lived Terry Brown and Bob Diechen who also owned a dragster. When we met them, they were racing what was Tony Densham's old 'Worden' dragster, but they were in the process of building a 'competition-altered' class dragster using the larger four-and-a-half-litre version of the Daimler V8 engine. A year or two later, American Autoparts opened up across the road from our shop - which was at the top of Melbourne Road where Terry and Bob lived. So, within the space of five parallel streets, were three dragster owners and a speed shop. In adjacent Carshalton was 'Mike the Pipe', an exhaust specialist who at the time supplied the majority of drag racers in England. Finally, a stone's throw from there, was Tony Densham's Sutton Rebore, which was not only a machine shop, but also the home of the fastest and quickest dragster in the UK. I'm not sure there was anywhere else in the country with such a concentration of drag racing enthusiasts, and all of these people were instrumental in my early years of the sport.

*   *   *

I stripped the two-and-a-half-litre Daimler engine down and rebuilt it with Dad. I'd had some engine building experience already as he used to allow me to tear apart various small engines on such things like mopeds, a Peel three-wheeler (now very rare and desirable!), and even the lawn mower.[3] I'd been involved with servicing the kart motor too, but this was on a whole new level.

We decided to use the motor as standard with no modifications, just build it well to original tolerances (known as blueprinting). I polished everything, inside and out. The ports, the connecting rod

---

[3] *Our Suffolk Punch lawn mower was self-propelled and I made a board on two wheels to tow behind it and stand on instead of walk - we ended up having two of these and racing them around the garden.*

beams, the rocker arm covers - the lot. We had the rotating assembly balanced, and assembled it with care. Dad used his engineering skills and connections to roll up a purpose made steel bellhousing, which also adapted the engine to the Ford Thames three-speed gearbox. Pretty much everything was purpose made or refurbished used parts, even the fuel tank was repurposed from a cement mixer. The only brand-new parts I remember us buying was a pair of Wolfrace wheels, which were wrapped in a pair of part-worn tyres from a Lola racing car.

Our good friend John Penfold was the roadie for the rock and roll band The Wild Angels, and it seemed that 'Wild Angel' was a suitable name for the car, a name that was sign written on the cowl by an old school friend, Mike Charman. In 1974, before we'd even driven the car, it was displayed at both the Crystal Palace and Belle Vue Manchester Custom Car shows. This was a good tie-in for The Wild Angels as they'd just released their latest album 'Out at Last', so the car was used to aid publicity.

An early trip to Blackbushe with 'The Wild Angel' dragster. L to R: Debbie, Me, Mum, and Dad

I turned seventeen in January, and passed my driving test in April - first time - and entered the first available drag race we could - at Blackbushe Aerodrome near Camberley. As no one really knew who we were, me and Dad actually took turns in driving the car, and what with fireproof balaclava, goggles and a crash helmet on, no-one could really tell who was driving! You couldn't get away with that now.

In the '70s dragsters were push started. Here's Dick's PA Cresta being pressed into service

Apart from discovering that we really needed to use all three gears in the gearbox, all went well. With that sorted and no more than a re-paint, we continued to race the car in that form until 1977. I believe it went as fast as 12.9 seconds in the quarter mile, but I really can't be sure and sadly, have no records.

Towards the end of that year we decided that we'd build a new car for the Competition Altered class. I can't recall what triggered this, but Wild Angel was sold, a fibreglass one-piece Fiat Topolino body purchased from fellow drag racer Pat Cuss, and another Daimler engine found in Curley's scrap yard - this time from a Daimler SP250 Dart - yes, a very rare and desirable car now. Having looked at many competition-altered cars, we drew up a full-size plan on a large sheet of shuttering plywood atop the three-quarter size billiard table in our (what was to be and yet to be decorated), lounge. We bought the tube, had the necessary bends formed by Mike the Pipe, and proceeded to cut, notch and tack weld together the frame. This was then taken to my uncle's factory where their skilled welder finish-welded the chassis. A rear axle from an Austin Westminster was pulled from a pile of axles in Curley's yard and narrowed by Dad, again at his brother's factory, and fitted with the required gear ratio taken from a London taxi cab.

Once again, I was polishing everything on the Daimler motor to within an inch of its life, and a new bellhousing had been formed (in aluminium this time), when a Chevrolet 283ci V8 became available along with a four-speed 'Muncie' gearbox - an opportunity too good to miss. This motor was purchased and the Daimler sold on. We rebuilt the Chevy motor in its stock form - just paying attention to detail as usual and the car was completed, but we decided against continuing with the Wild Angel moniker.

My best mate Dick was working as a roadie for a band called Rough Diamonds at the time, and for no other reason than the name Rough Diamond Racing sounded right, that's what we decided to call the new car. The body was painted pale blue by a local accident repair centre, Mike got involved again and cut the vinyl 'sign writing' by hand and applied it to the nose of the car and we were ready to go racing. Shortly after the name was chosen, there was a legal battle between 'our' band Rough Diamonds, and another band of the same title for the use of the name. The other side won, and Dick was now a roadie for The Speedometers (yes, that is the correct spelling). But for me the Rough Diamond name stuck. Little did I know then that the name would still be with me today!

Initially we tried running a twin carburettor and manifold set-up that we'd bought from a fellow racer, but it soon transpired on the first outing with the car it wasn't compatible and we couldn't make it run properly - lack of experience might have had something to do with it too. So, we borrowed a manifold and carburettor from Steve Thompson, a friend of American Autoparts and an American car specialist. This worked well, and we soon bought our own new Holley carb and a second-hand Chevrolet Corvette intake manifold.

In this form it was fun to drive, but over the winter of the following year, we rebuilt the front end to accommodate the more traditional torsion bar front suspension and lengthen the wheelbase to improve handling - not that handling had been an issue. A larger, but severely blown up, 327 cubic inch Chevrolet engine was found for the handsome sum of £15. This was rebuilt and the cylinder heads 'ported' to our best guess. After another trip to the USA, Dad brought back a racing torque converter and a manual valve body for the Power-glide transmission we'd acquired. This sort of setup was the route racers in the USA were taking, but the UK were lagging behind. Fortunately a little sponsorship from one of our hire shop customers (thank you Peter Pitts!), helped pay for parts that would normally be out of reach for me.

The Topolino at Snetterton

The 'Wild Angel' dragster at Blackbushe 1975

Photo: Mike Key

The 'Rough Diamond' Fiat Topolino at Santa Pod 1980

Photo: © Roger Gorringe

We continued to run the Topolino with this set-up, when a trip to the USA at the end of 1979 (this time by myself and Dick) brought back more parts. I splashed out on a new intake manifold, a pair of used high performance cylinder heads, and a whole bunch of other stuff that we brought home in our suitcases. We nearly gave ourselves hernias carrying the bags through customs while trying to make it look like they were 'standard holiday' weight!

The Rough Diamond Topolino was again duly upgraded over the winter which resulted in performances in 1980 as quick as 9.8 seconds at 130mph, making it one of the fastest petrol powered normally aspirated drag race cars outside the USA. Dad rarely came to the races these days, I ran the car with Dick, and his cousin Paul 'Spunky' Mortimer[4]. We travelled the country to Santa Pod, Blackbushe, Snetterton race circuit, and one trip to Mainz Finthen in Germany. In Germany I met someone who would become a lifelong friend - but more of that later.

*   *   *

We were beginning to take things quite seriously now, but always within a very tight budget. I'd been taught to be selective in what I purchased, and use the parts well in a 'combination' that made the most of what we had. But the trouble with drag racing is - you always want a bit more, to go a bit faster.

Fellow racer John Everitt had commissioned a new car to be built for him, but he'd run out of money, and fell out with the chassis builder, which meant he owned a part-built car that he wasn't able to finish. The design was super low and very much in the style of the new cars racing in the USA. It was little more than a bunch of tubing tack welded together, a front axle, and a pre-loved fibreglass Ford Model T body that didn't fit and hadn't been

---

[4] *John Price, the Santa Pod Commentator, bestowed me the nickname 'Funky' after the Goodies novelty song 'The Funky Gibbon' and it happened to rhyme with Paul's nickname Spunky. When Tony Morris began driving my old car, noticing that Tony was slightly more well-built than me, John named him 'Chunky' - a name that sticks with him today.*

mounted. But John was keen to get racing again, so we struck a deal - a swap for my rolling chassis with his unfinished pile of parts. I kept the engine and transmission from the Topolino. When I got back from collecting the new 'car' Dad was somewhat underwhelmed - he couldn't really see my vision, or understand why I'd swapped a perfectly good and usable race car for what was in essence a lot of work to do. As for the Topolino, it was stolen from John's garage before he got to drive it and never seen again.

Over the winter of 1980/81 we completed that 'lot of work', and produced what I thought was the most up to date and modern looking competition-altered in the UK. With the motor from the previous car installed, a much stronger rear axle than the one used in the Topolino, and bigger slicks, it looked awesome! But running the old engine with no real upgrades it wasn't actually much faster than the Topo, the only real concession to making it quicker was the installation of a 'transmission brake' for improved starts - but damn it looked good!

1981 came and went, and 1982 saw the fitting of a nitrous oxide injection kit from Bob Hatton. Nitrous oxide was a fairly recent development in performance upgrade in the UK, and few people had managed to use it successfully without hurting parts. Careful selection of components, a judicious approach, and some safety features, saw what I believe was the first truly *successful* use of nitrous on a race car in the UK - in that we had no damage to the motor.

Gradually, upgrades were made to improve performance and reliability, a wing added to help stability at speed, and at the end of 1983, an increase in the quantity of nitrous oxide used culminated in Rough Diamond holding both ends of the 'D Comp. Altered' class record at 8.89 seconds and 151mph.

That winter saw a repaint as the body was looking a bit tired after three years of racing (and a couple of flame burnouts), and it was changed a little to allow space for potential sponsorship logos.

We hit the track again at Easter 1984 with the fresh-looking car, and then Alan Reitmeister, in his top fuel dragster, hit the Armco

The 'Rough Diamond' Ford Model 'T' at Santa Pod 1981

Photo: © Roger Gorringe

barrier hard not too far from the start line and died instantly. I put our car back on the trailer and we came home. I didn't know Alan well, in fact we had both been on the same flight home from the USA a few weeks before and spoke then. Although his car was a much more powerful machine than mine, he wasn't going as fast as my car was capable of at the time of the crash.

There hadn't been many fatalities in UK drag racing, but I'd been present for all of them so far, and it played on my mind. A couple of days later I was out with Dick and our girlfriends for the evening, and while we were driving toward Croydon High Street I decided to quit racing, and said so there and then - Dick seemed to take the news quite hard.

*   *   *

A few years younger than me, Trevor Cox was Wallington's answer to Burt Reynolds. Dark hair, with a broad grin, and a bushy moustache to rival my own, he drove a Pontiac Trans Am just like the one in *Smokey and the Bandit*. If you'd seen me and Trevor together, we would have looked like a cut price (and shorter) version of Burt Reynolds and Tom Selleck - or The Mario Kart Brothers!

43

To Trevor, the accelerator pedal was not an item with which to modulate your speed, but a device that took a vehicle from stationary to maximum speed in the shortest possible time. Every passenger ride with Trev would be a buttock clenching ordeal, and the Trans Am being left-hand drive, the passenger got to see the potential accident first. He used to ride motorbikes too, in fact how on earth he's still with us is beyond me.

In 1983 radio DJ and TV presenter Noel Edmonds presented a Saturday evening prime-time BBC television show called *The Late, Late Breakfast Show*, and on one show they screened stuntwoman Jacquie de Creed making an (apparently), record-breaking car jump. It was filmed at Santa Pod where she drove a Ford Mustang up a ramp, then 'flying' as far as possible before landing on a row of old parked cars. This led to a challenge to the public to do the same - it would be aired live on the BBC show. Trevor fancied some of this action, and told me and Dick just that. We considered the idea for all of two minutes, and hatched a plan.

We only had a couple of weeks to prepare for Trevor's record attempt. Clearly the car needed to be fast, preferably with a V8 engine, as well as being relatively cheap. Dick's now ex-girlfriend, Sandy, had just the car - a 1966 Chevy Malibu station wagon - and it was for sale. Dick arranged the deal on Trevor's behalf, while not letting on for what Sandy's beloved Chevy was destined…

Between the challenge being set and the shooting day, there was a production meeting held at Santa Pod. Trev, Dick and myself bundled into the Trans Am and set sail. With the throttle almost pegged to the floor on the motorway, we came up behind a car that simply wouldn't let us pass, with the driver gesticulating furiously. Obviously, this was of some frustration to Trevor, but finally, the driver of the car in front relented and pulled over to let us by. And as we passed the unhappy driver pressed his police warrant card to the side window. 'Wanker!' shouted Trevor, and we continued to devour the M1 at no insignificant speed.

With the Chevy Malibu in my parents' driveway in front of my workshop all manner of friends pitched in to prepare the car. All of the interior and any excess weight was stripped out, and a mutual friend, 'Big' Si Pritchard (who wasn't big in any way whatsoever), bent up and welded in a substantial roll-cage made from scaffold tubing.

I temporarily robbed my race car of its nitrous oxide system, and installed it on the Chevy which would add an additional seventy-five horsepower at the flip of a switch. My parents were away in California at the time, so the work on the 'flying car' took on a party atmosphere generating a lot of interest from friends and locals.

We towed the car to Santa Pod using my Chevy El Camino tow-truck and trailer, and being regulars to the venue, I parked a large old caravan there permanently, which was our accommodation and base when we were racing.

I think there were four 'competitors' vying to beat Jacquie de Creed's record. The stunt team checked the cars over to make sure they were as safe as possible and Noel Edmonds flew in in his helicopter to check things out in the morning, wished everyone luck and flew off again.

Noel's fellow radio DJ John Peel, and actress Sandra Dickinson, were on hand to carry out interviews and present the live elements of the show. A long ramp had been built on the back of some articulated lorry trailers parked end to end, after which there was a row of scrap cars on which the flying cars would land. This was all located in Santa Pod's shutdown area beyond the quarter mile finish line, meaning the cars would have almost half a mile in which to build up speed.

With a running order chosen, the idea would be that a car would tackle the jump live on TV. John Peel would provide the commentary and 'throw' back to the studio while the car was removed and everything reset.

Trevor was the second contender. We left him at the start line waiting for the signal to go, while Dick and I waited next to the landing area to assist if needed. With the cameras rolling, Trevor switched on the accelerator in his usual fashion, hit the nitrous oxide switch, and made his way up the track. Unfortunately, there

Trevor Cox with the 'Pedal to the metal'

was slight misfire that impacted his speed a little, but he was clearly going at a fair lick when he hit the ramp. The car flew a good distance and landed on the old bangers beneath. The safety crew got Trevor out of the car while I shut the valve on the nitrous cylinder.

On landing the steering column was pushed back into the car, causing the steering wheel to come into full contact with Trevor. His full-face crash helmet subsequently made contact with his nose, resulting in a sore nose and a nosebleed. Where the wheel hit his chest it made full contact with a St. Christopher's medal, forming a perfect imprint of the Saint on his chest. The distance 'flown'

The Malibu steering wheel, stamped with date and distance

by the Malibu was 139 feet - unfortunately short of the record number[5]. Dick still has the steering wheel.

(Watching at home, live on TV, was Sandy, whose treasured Chevy had just been well and truly trashed. This was the first she knew of it, and it would be years before she would speak to either me or Dick again).

Next up was a chap in a Ford Escort. He attacked the ramp hard and took off, then gravity had its way, bringing the car onto the edge of the line of bangers, causing the car to cart wheel end over end along the track between the landing area and the Armco barrier, distributing parts of Ford Escort hither and thither. Spectators dived for cover while mangled parts of Dagenham's finest narrowly missed John Peel and the cameraman.

The driver was pretty shaken up, but thankfully uninjured, nor fortunately were any of the spectators. The debris was cleared up ready for the final attempt - the one expected to be most likely to succeed.

Rich Smith was driving a Jensen Interceptor, and with its 7.2 litre American Chrysler V8, it was easily the most powerful car in attendance. With the live airtime thrown back to the track, Rich was given the signal to go, and powered down the dragstrip. Clearly travelling at great speed, he tackled the ramp and flew from its end, but with the huge weight of the large V8 engine up front, the car nose-dived into the parked cars, and flipped end over end, ripping itself completely apart.

The passenger compartment came to rest upside down roughly next to where I was standing, while the engine and axle were scattered like discarded toys along the track surface. I saw something pouring down over the inverted driver, which to me initially looked like blood but turned out to be sand from one of

---

[5] *Trevor was convinced that he had what it took to break the record, and went on to purpose-build a Chevrolet powered Opel Manta for the attempt - a project in which I had no hand. The car was completed, and he sought sponsorship, but sadly, the project literally never got off the ground.*

the bags he'd used to help balance the car's weight - clearly it hadn't worked.

The live broadcast quickly 'threw back' to the studio, where a shell-shocked Noel Edmonds wrapped up the show. Emergency services were on hand quickly to remove Rick from the car, and transported him to hospital. He suffered a broken neck, along with damage to his head, back and pelvis. The injuries would see him wheelchair bound for life[6].

The remains of the Jensen

Both the police and press now arrived, and wrapping things up after this was clearly a subdued affair. Our team retired back to the relative comfort of my caravan, where we were soon joined by John Peel and Sandra Dickinson, both of whom basically wanted somewhere to hide.

Between us we finished off a couple of bottles of Jack Daniels.

*   *   *

---

[6] *The Late, Late Breakfast show later incurred an injury to a woman's shoulder while being fired from a cannon, and later a man would be killed while preparing to complete a bungee jump from an exploding box stunt. The show was subsequently cancelled.*

I put Rough Diamond up for sale and hoped for sufficient funds to buy a decent road car. It took a while to sell, but it sold to Tony Morris, an Englishman living in Germany who I'd met at Mainz Finthen when I'd raced the Topolino. Well I say sold, I actually exchanged it for a Chevy Blazer 4WD, a big block Chevrolet motor and £500. I sold the motor to fellow racer Dave Mingay, and eventually sold the Blazer. I used the £500 to put towards building a Beach Buggy, which I did on a whim after a neighbour put their VW Beetle up for sale. It took ten days to build from start to finish. I sold this in November 1984 and I now had £4,750 burning a hole in my pocket.

Exchange and Mart was the way most used cars were bought and sold in those days, and so I looked at a couple Corvettes, and I even considered a Ferrari Dino which was only just out of my reach, as was a Monteverdi previously owned by John Entwistle of The Who. Then, just after Christmas I happened to be in conversation with Peter Hemmings, a motor technician specialising in luxury vehicles - he knew of a Corvette that he serviced that was up for sale. On the 6th January 1985, I drew every penny I owned from the building society account in cash, taking it with me to a shop called Mr. Light in New King's Road Chelsea. I handed the money over and drove away in a 1978

Handing over every penny I had

Silver Anniversary Chevrolet Corvette. A car I still have to this very day!

There I was, twenty-seven years old, and tooling about in a 'Vette. Life was good.

*   *   *

Being a good four inches taller than me, Tony needed the roll cage and steering cross-member of Rough Diamond changed to suit his size. I did this as part of the deal, and Tony returned to the UK in November to race the car at the Fireworks Meet at Santa Pod before taking it back to Germany.

Soon after Tony brought the car back to the UK for the Easter meet, where Dick and I would serve as crew, I got the call that would see me leave for the USA as a crew member on Jim Head's Top Fuel Funny Car team. See chapter nine for that story.

When I returned to the UK towards the end of the year, I continued to crew for Tony whenever I could, occasionally travelling to Holland and Germany to do so. After six years of use, during which I built a new alcohol-injected and nitrous equipped motor for the car, along with various other modifications for Tony, he sold the dragster on and eventually it disappeared. But again, more on that story later.

Apart from helping good friend Ron Pudney Jnr. prepare and race a Chevy Monza race car for the Super Gas class, a spell followed where I wasn't actively involved with running or owning a race car. Then in 1995, when Alli turned thirty years of age, I made what was perhaps a mistake, by buying her a day's racing tuition at Brands Hatch for her birthday. Another day, then another followed. She was being taught in a Formula First car, which was an entry level single-seat race car, but this led me to look into what sort of racing might be possible; without any real intentions, but a sort of 'feasibility study'. The enthusiast magazine *Cars and Car Conversions* carried a feature about 'sprinting', a motor sport discipline of which I was barely familiar.

The article featured a variety of cars to demonstrate the sport, including a Mini saloon car and a Formula Ford. It also included a calendar of events - a few days later Alli and me went to the very next one listed, at Goodwood.

Not only was there a more relaxed attitude to motor racing, we were also struck by the 'non-spectator' element. Sprinting is not usually deemed to be a spectator sport, and entry to the track is usually free. We also saw the Mini and the Formula Ford that had been featured in *Cars and Car Conversions*. We struck up conversation with the owners of the Formula Ford - Neville and Tina Moon, a delightful couple (whom we remain in touch with today), who shared the driving of the car. This was beginning to look interesting.

'Sprinting' is timed laps around a track, and only one car is on the track at any time (or spaced apart so they shouldn't catch each other - overtaking is not allowed), so a second driver can swap into the same car and compete in the same class - and against the other driver. We were told that Formula Ford cars could be bought for around £3,000. We had access to £3,000.

The Formula Ford Festival at Brands Hatch was in October, so of course we went 'just to have a look'. Old habits die hard, and a week later I was driving to Grimsby to collect our Van Diemen RF87 Formula Ford race car - complete with trailer.

I rebuilt the car over the winter of '95 and early '96, and with no practice, testing, or any other experience, we entered the first sprint event of the season at Goodwood. The only concession we made to prepare ourselves was to go there the day before to walk and cycle the track.

We caused a bit of a stir, as in preparing the car, we'd brought some of the drag racing 'sensibility' to the design of the paintwork. Based around the now usual 'Rough Diamond Blue' (actually Ford Olympic blue), and our friend Neil Melliard painted a design like no other seen in sprinting before - the car looked stunning.

In spite of a slight ignition misfire, I managed to place third in class at that first event, and I seem to remember Alli was fourth or fifth. We were hooked. For me the discipline - getting the best out of your car and yourself, without the distraction of having other cars around you to avoid or crash into - was intoxicating. It was a bit like drag racing with corners. What's more, we appeared to be quite good at it!

The Formula Ford was enormous fun to drive, reliable, and easy to maintain. Running costs and entry fees were reasonable too. We'd occasionally go further afield, but Goodwood, Lydden and North Weald were possible to get to and from in a day. It was rare that we'd come home without an award, one or other or both of us would often achieve top three in class, and Alli was frequently the fastest lady. She became a skilful driver, often beating me in the wet.

The highlights in the first three years of sprinting was Alli winning British Women's Racing Drivers Club Sprint Championship, and I won the 1998 All Circuit Sprint championship. We also got to be on Sky News for a feature on women racing drivers.

We decided to bite the bullet and move up a class for 1999 and bought a Vauxhall Lotus single-seater, which is a proper 'slicks and wings' machine that previously raced in the one-make championship. Initially, apart from painting the car in Rough Diamond blue, we ran it in its standard form. We loved the extra speed and performance the two-litre engine gave us, and the additional grip from the aero and tyres induced confidence. With upgrades to the engine and larger wheels and tyres we soon found the limits of the chassis, the design of which was unusual and became a limiting factor in how fast the car would go. Nevertheless, overall fastest time of day awards followed for both of us, with Alli having the distinction of being the only woman (as far as we know), to win an FTD (Fastest Time of the Day), at Goodwood.

We'd been competing at the historic Brighton Speed Trials in the Formula Ford, and continued to do so in the Vauxhall Lotus. Neither of these cars were competitive at this event, but it was a fun day's racing in a straight line over a quarter of a mile along the beachfront Madeira Drive - much like drag racing. You also got to meet like-minded people from other motor sport disciplines that you wouldn't normally get to meet.

At the 2000 event I spotted a car I knew from drag racing, a Dodge Dart that ran in the Super Gas class. As the speed trials were on during the same weekend as the drag racing world finals at Santa Pod, I poked my nose in to enquire why they were here - and not there. The story was that they had qualified at Santa Pod on the Friday, had driven down here to race at the trials, and were to drive back to Santa Pod for eliminations on Sunday. 'That's keen,' I thought.

'How's it going?' I asked the crewmember I'd engaged in conversation. 'Well, we've got a bit of a problem - our driver's drag race licence isn't acceptable. He needs a speed licence. He's off now looking for someone who's got the right sort of licence and knows how to drive a drag race car.'

I literally put my hand in the air and said, 'That'll be me then!'

'What? You've driven drag race cars?'

'Yep, an eight second Comp. Altered.'

'Come with me.'.

The chap took me to the car's owner, Paul Marston.

'This fella drives dragsters,' he said with an unnecessary degree of enthusiasm.

A conversation followed between me and Paul. He remembered me from earlier years, and the Rough Diamond altered, and was more than content that I knew my way about a car such as his. We went to the organisers and changed the entry to my name. I was now driving two cars at the same event - ours and 'Grumpy's Dodge'. It would mean some logistical challenges, but nothing we couldn't manage.

The speed trials spectators weren't used to seeing cars perform a static line-lock burnout - where the front brakes are locked so the rear tyres can spin to heat them up. They loved it. On my first practice run I was trying to get a feel for the car, and pretty much smoked the tyres the entire length of the track. My subsequent two-timed runs went much better, and every time I drove the car back down the track to the pits the crowd were cheering and waving over the railings from the road above Madeira Drive.

In Grumpy's seat for the first time at the Brighton Speed trials

We managed to get the Dodge into the top six run off - the fastest six cars would get an extra timed run to decide the fastest time of day over all. While just missing out on the FTD, we finished third fastest overall, the fastest in the Sports Libre class (re-setting the class record in the process), and won the award for the fastest 'push rod' engine-vehicle (engines whose valve gear is operated by pushrods rather than by overhead cams).

It wasn't the top award of the meet, but we'd left an impression. And instigated a firm and lasting friendship with Paul.

Paul went on to compete at a few sprint events in his road car just to get the required signatures for a speed licence so he could return to Brighton and compete - this time in his new Chrysler 'PT Bruiser'. An arrangement was made for Alli to drive Grumpy's Dodge in an effort to win the Fastest Lady Award. Paul gave Alli some training in the Dodge at a 'run-what-ya-brung' drag race event at North Weald, and got to grips with the car quite quickly.

We all rocked up to Brighton for the speed trials in 2001, Paul in 'The Bruiser' and Alli in 'Grumpy'. I was content to just crew and look after Alli in the car. Again, the crowd loved the drag race cars. Paul took FTD, and Alli managed a top six finish, but sadly, missed out on the fastest lady award.

The following year Paul went back to Brighton with only the Bruiser, and successfully defended his FTD award. But the writing was on the wall for drag-race type vehicles at Brighton, the organisers were nervous about the power and unpredictability of the handling - they're not designed to run on a public road. There was already a restriction on single-seat racing cars to a maximum of two litres, so 2002 was the last time they would allow vehicles primarily designed for drag racing to compete. Drag racing has always been a brash misunderstood form of motorsport, so I think too that there was an element of class distinction. The event is a prestigious historic event, and many of the entrants are wealthy historic racers, and I don't think that drag racers were deemed to be 'the right sort of people'.

*   *   *

Alli and I had competed in about twenty sprint events by the end of 2001 - it was relentless, and on our way home from the last event I simply said to Alli, 'I don't think I can do this anymore.' 'Nor me,' she replied.

We put the car up for sale.

The following April we part exchanged the Vauxhall Lotus for a Caterham Seven, the logic being that at least we could use the car on the road, and have a bit of fun with it if we felt like taking it to a sprint. Alli ended up competing at a couple of sprints, and we both drove it at the Brighton Speed Trials, but we stayed true to our word and didn't get back on the band-wagon. Except...

*   *   *

We were well acquainted with Owen and Tony of Jade Motorsport, manufacturer of Jade sports prototype racing cars -

they used to perform the alignment and suspension set-ups on our sprint cars. Owen was quite keen to get the name Jade in front of more people - and Brighton seemed a logical place to do so. I suggested that perhaps Alli and me could double drive the Jade Trackstar at the 2003 Speed Trials. Fitted with a powerful Chrysler V6, it was a formidably quick car on the circuit, and the thoughts were that it might be in with a chance for the ladies FTD or even overall FTD.

With its sequential six-speed gearbox and gobs of power we might have been right - it was a shame that lower gear ratios hadn't been selected and put in the gearbox as I suggested. Once again, neither of us quite managed to achieve for which we set out. It was though, loads of fun to drive and received a good deal of attention. In 2010 Alli got yet one more chance for Brighton glory.

Alli in Steve Broughton's SBD OMS at the Brighton Speed Trials

Steve Broughton had been building performance engines for race cars for many years, and competed in a variety of cars and classes. We'd bought tuning equipment from him for both the Vauxhall Lotus and the Caterham. His main ride and passion at the time was an OMS - a small lightweight single-seat race car powered by a Suzuki Hayabusa motorcycle engine - only he'd supercharged this one.

For a small consideration he handed the seat to Alli for Brighton. The power to weight ratio wasn't far short of that of a Formula one car and really did stand a chance of doing more than rather well.

Steve was nearly a foot taller than Alli, so I made the necessary adjustments to the car to make it fit her, and Alli got used to the car in the car park of the trading estate where Steve's business was based in Surbiton. The day started well with Alli being the fastest during practice - and then it rained. Getting the car off of the start line was a challenge, and the damp conditions benefited the less powerful cars. Once again, our efforts were thwarted.

*   *   *

Rewind to 2003 and Paul Marston asked me to join him on a road trip to Toulouse to look at a Competition-Altered dragster that he was thinking of buying - primarily for the engine. We jumped in his van and set off. The car, known as 'The Alien', was built in France by Bertrand Duboit, and was clearly worth every Euro he was asking for it, so we loaded it up and brought it back to the UK.

The plan was to pull the engine and transmission from the dragster and sell the rolling chassis on, but on closer inspection we deemed it to be too good a car to split up. The only problem was, Paul was too tall to get into it. We struck a deal that I would give the car once over and prep it for racing - and in return I would get to drive it. This would put the car in front of potential buyers.

In August we took The Alien to Shakespeare County Raceway. It was an animal of a car to drive, and while I got knocked out of eliminations early, I managed to record a best time and speed of 7.82 seconds at 178mph - the quickest I had gone in a dragster.

The following May we took the car to Santa Pod, where once again I drove it for Paul, however the performance was just shy of what we'd managed the year before. Paul had several other cars that he raced, and decided to park the Altered for the rest of the year while we decided what to do next, but one way or another he was going to keep the car and we'd find a way for me to drive it again in 2005.

In January of that year, Alli was pregnant with Scott, and I was decorating the outside of the house. I fell off the scaffold and broke my back. Not only was this more than trifle inconvenient for

Driving 'The Alien' at Santa Pod

Photo: Ivan Sansom

a whole host of reasons, it meant that I wasn't going to be able to drive for Paul as hoped. My old friend John Everitt (with whom I'd swapped chassis back in 1980), was without a car or a drive, so jumped in the seat instead. Eventually he would buy the car from Paul.

Apart from occasionally helping out Paul (and those one-off visits to Brighton), I kept myself pretty much out of the motor sport world. Fortunately, I'd recovered well from my back injury, Alli had given birth to Scott, both my parents had passed away, and in 2007 we moved house from Wallington to a small village near Canterbury.

5

Viennese quick step

So here I was at Dover docks early in 2008 on a winter's morning being overcharged for two coffees and a tea at the Costa. I was with Dick, and another friend Maurice Takoor - who'd not met each other until this very morning. Maurice was a hot rod enthusiast I'd known for many years, and a stalwart of the National Street Rod Association. He'd also been instrumental in the setting up Santa Pod drag strip when it was established in the 1960s.

We were killing time before boarding the ferry to Calais, and outside was Maurice's Mercedes Viano towing an enclosed trailer that I'd bought a couple of weeks previously. We were heading for Vienna, and hoping to get there and back before the forecasted snow.

It was Tony Morris' fault. He'd been wondering what had happened to our old Competition-Altered, the one that we both had owned and raced, and which had apparently disappeared from the face of the earth. Having left Germany for the more drag race friendly climate of Florida, his sister Andrea was still living in Germany, and remained connected with the drag racing scene there, so Tony asked her to make enquiries.

The trouble with 'making enquiries' is that you might find exactly what you were looking for, and so it transpired. Andrea discovered that the car was now owned by Guenter Duacsek, and having bought it from where it was resting behind a discotheque in Germany (where at one time it had been on display in the foyer), it was now with him just outside Vienna. Tony's next mistake was asking 'Does he want to sell it?'

To be fair, Guenter wasn't too bothered, but a price was mentioned, and considering the neglected condition of the car, complete with its dummy engine and lurid paintwork including murals depicting scantily clad women, it was a fair price.

Tony's thought was that he and I could buy the car between us. I'd keep it in the UK, and when he was visiting he would be able to race it, and so could I at other times if I wished. As plans go, it wasn't too outrageous - and then Tony's wife Lynn brought him to his senses. Clearly spending money on a car that lived 4,500 miles away, and that he would only get to use perhaps once a year, wasn't, she suggested, perhaps the best use of their money.

I however, remained smitten with the idea of bringing my old race car back to life, and so it was that we found ourselves drinking the most expensive hot drinks in the country waiting to board a ferry.

Fortunately, Maurice and Dick got on, and would subsequently become firm friends (these days, thanks to the geography of where we all now live, they see more of each other than I do of either of them!). We were using Maurice's Mercedes as it would be much better on fuel than the Chevy Blazer I otherwise would have used, and it seemed appropriate that Dick came along to not only help share the driving, but being my crew chief during all the years I raced, I was adamant that he should be involved in the repatriation of 'our car'.

We made a blistering pace, found Guenter and the car, handed over the Euros and loaded up the car. Slowed a little by a puncture we made haste, certainly driving faster than the law

Rough Diamond 'as found' in Austria – and Maurice

allowed for vehicles pulling a trailer - as several other road users indicated to us as they drove by.

So, on a whim, the car I had built twenty-eight years previously, was back in my own workshop. That bandwagon I'd been avoiding was just over the horizon.

*　　　*　　　*

To be fair, it was a casual re-immersion into the sport. I was in no rush, but I established that to race in national events there would have to be a *lot* of changes. Primarily the driver's area of the chassis was not up to modern standards, and unless I upgraded I would be relegated to only being able to drive the car at 'run-what-ya-brung' events, and that didn't really appeal. I bit the bullet, and decided to fabricate a whole new chassis for the car up to spec, but duplicating the original as much as I could incorporating as many of the original parts as possible. It would be a 'trigger's broom'[7] of a car. I made a start.

Then, breast cancer - the story of which is detailed later on in these pages. (Spoiler alert - she gets better!). Alli's diagnosis threw our world into a spin, a spin that is unimaginable unless you've been through it. But it made us re-evaluate what's important and focus our attention. Rebuilding my old race car was a long way down that list.

But rebuild Rough Diamond we did. It took a while, buying parts and materials as we went along, with the decision to install a big block Chevy engine instead of the small block Chevy I used to run. The best times I ran were nitrous assisted, and I didn't want the inconvenience, potential engine damage, and lack of consistency that a nitrous motor possesses. A big block would provide similar times and speeds but with less exertion on the mechanical parts.

Paul Marston initially lent me a motor to use. He supplied it dismantled and I assembled it at my own expense; later I paid for it in full. Tony Morris donated a torque converter he no longer

---

[7] *When I was a kid, anything that had been modified or changed substantially during its life was described as a 'Grandad's broom', the inference being that grandad always had the same broom - though it had been fitted with two new handles and three new heads, it was still the same broom. Years later in the TV show Only Fools and Horses, the character Trigger - a road sweeper - described his own broom this way, and the expression 'Trigger's broom' has fallen into common parlance.*

Same car, same driver, same place – thirty-seven years part.

*The top photo was taken by fellow racer Jon Giles (spectating as a youngster) in 1981, the lower photo was shot by
Tony Morris in 2018.*

needed, and my good friend, sign-writer Neil Melliard, duplicated the original lettering on the car using old photographs for reference.

With Dick, Maurice, Alli and a five-year-old Scott as crew, I chose the Easter meet of 2011 to debut the car in the 'Super-Pro' class. Taking advantage of a test day the day before the event to 'settle myself back in', we went on to unexpectedly qualify in the number one position, and subsequently got knocked out in the semi-finals. The times and speeds were bang on the money to where we were when I ran the car twenty-seven years earlier. The band-wagon I'd been avoiding was looking significantly larger.

*   *   *

If you saw someone drive their dragster to the start line, have the crew pour petrol over the tyres and the ground around them, then set fire to it while the driver calmly sits there, you might be tempted to call the men in white coats.

Yes, I did that - more than once!!

Getting the maximum amount of traction is key to drag racing. During the early drag race days in the USA someone had the bright idea of spinning the tyres in a pool of burning petrol in order to warm up the rubber, and as it happened - it worked, but the by product was that it was quite spectacular. Obviously, the idea moved to the UK, and back in 1984 I was one of those that performed 'flame burnouts' at night-time races. Soon after, the engine died on a car as the driver hit the throttle, leaving him sitting in a burning car. The flames were extinguished with no harm to the driver and little damage to the car, but the writing was on the wall - flame burnouts were actually quite dangerous - and banned. Soon after, the USA sanctioning bodies followed suit.

Move to Dragstalgia 2012, when the nostalgia drag race scene was getting off of the ground, and people wanted to race 'like how it was in the good old days.' Someone had the bright idea of resurrecting flame burnouts as a spectacle, but this time with our excellent fire and safety crew standing close by. It must have taken all of a nanosecond for me to say, 'Yep, I'll do that.'

Rough Diamond and three other cars lined up to entertain the crowd with something most of them had never seen before. After a full safety briefing, friend and well- known engine builder Rob Loaring was tasked with laying down the petrol and setting it on fire. I could feel the warmth and see the orange glow as the flames licked around the back of the car, I got the nod to mat the throttle. The tyres span furiously throwing the burning fuel high into the air. The crowd loved it, and just for a short while we four drivers were heroes. Yes, there was a little damage to the paint (let's just call them battle scars), but like my Dad before me when taking his hydro over a ski ramp, I wanted to do it again. I'd go on to perform flame burnouts at several events after that.

I've got some excellent photographs.

*   *   *

Towards the tail end of 2008, Alli was in recovery of her cancer treatment, and we decided to have a day out and watch a sprint at Lydden Hill circuit, which, having moved to Kent, was now only a twenty-minute drive away.

We spent some time catching up with some of our old sprinting friends, and were particularly taken by a couple of single-seat racing cars. Then I made the mistake of verbalising my thoughts, 'We should do this again,' I said to Alli. My thinking was that having been through such a torrid time, it might be nice for Alli to have some fun again. She didn't immediately say 'Great idea,' but she didn't say no either.

With a trailer in tow I found myself travelling to Wellingborough - bizarrely close to Santa Pod. I pushed a wad of money into a man's hand and loaded into the trailer a 395 Dallara. Yes, a genuine Formula Three car.

This was the real deal, a proper carbon tub single-seat race car, the same model of race car that many drivers cut their teeth in before stepping up to F1 - including the likes of Ralf Schumacher. It was powered by a two litre Vauxhall motor with the F3

This is what a flame burnout should look like!

Photo: Matt Woods

The downside of performing a flame burnout – battle scars!

Dave and Dick trying to pretend that they haven't noticed Jon taking a photograph, while Maurice waits patiently to run his vintage dragster 'Spirit'

Photo: Jon Spoard

Team Rough Diamond 2018. L to R Dick, Maurice, Dave, Alli, Tony

Photo: Jon Spoard

Launching hard from the start line in 2018 with Alli looking on

Photo: Jon Spoard

The three 'Team Rough Diamond' race cars

mandated restrictive fuel injection swapped for carburettors. A beautifully engineered car with effective aero, but with slightly less power than our previous Vauxhall Lotus, it was to be a very quick drive. On longer tracks like Goodwood, 160mph.

I went through the car and changed a few things to my liking, asked Jade Motorsport to set up the suspension and alignment, painted it Rough Diamond blue and went sprinting again. We now had two band-wagons looming over the horizon...

It seemed that neither of us had lost our pace, and managed a few good placings, although an FTD never came our way in this car. Restricting ourselves to Lydden and Goodwood for convenience, and between sprinting and drag racing we were having quite a lot of fun. But in June 2012 Alli entered a sprint at Lydden, and as I drove the Dallara to scrutineering I noticed the engine wasn't running properly. It passed tech but I couldn't get to the bottom of the problem - practice had begun and time was running out. To my immense disappointment I failed, we loaded the car up and I put the car in the naughty corner - where it has stayed ever since. At time of writing it's still there, and remains 'unfinished business.'

Alli fully committed in the Dallara exiting the chicane at Goodwood

*   *   *

I continued with the dragster but not with great commitment, although by now we owned a proper 7.5 tonne 'race truck' to haul whichever car we were racing, and a caravan to stay in at the track - hotels were both expensive and booked up on most race weekends. At the end of May 2013, we found ourselves at Santa Pod's 'Main Event' with the Altered.

We were towing the car to the start line behind Maurice's van, and whilst chatting to a friend while walking alongside the race car with my hand guiding the steering, my heel got caught under the rear tyre. It dragged me down and by the time Maurice was alerted and stopped, the full weight of the race car was on my feet - one on top of the other.

The injuries to both feet put me in a wheelchair for two months, and certainly put paid to my driving any sort of race car for the rest of the year. Santa Pod kindly invited me to co-commentate with Colin Theobald at the increasingly popular Dragstalgia event in July, suggesting that a driver might add some colour to the proceedings. And then, in July 2013, Scott turned eight...

*   *   *

When Scott was six, we gave him the opportunity to try his hand at Bambino Karts at our local kart track, Buckmore Park. He took instruction well, and we looked quite hard at whether this was a direction we might go, but he didn't really have the pace of his contemporaries, and quite honestly, the uber-competitive nature[8] of some of the parents troubled me - many of them were investing heavily into the idea of their son or daughter being the next F1 champion, and while this of course can happen, we didn't want any part of it. So instead...

---

[8] *When I was racing karts as a junior, it wasn't uncommon to find the fathers arguing about the kids, sometimes ending up with a brawl on the infield. I remember one dad saying to another 'I'd punch you in the mouth, but I don't hit people wearing glasses.' To which he got the reply, 'I'll take them off and fight you from memory!'*

The day after Scott's eighth birthday we found ourselves at Santa Pod again (he went 'arrive and drive' karting on his birthday), alongside the junior dragster he was about to drive. Eight years of age is the youngest that kids can drive a dragster, and Santa Pod has a car that can be rented - along with tuition. Steve Seamarks showed Scott the ropes and allowed him a lot of runs. A couple of months later we rented the car again and entered Scott into his first race. To be honest, it wasn't great success as the car was terribly inconsistent and not at all well prepared, but most importantly, the next Gibbons generation was in the seat of a race car!

Towards the end of the year, when I was properly mobile again, I found myself at Jon Webster's workshop near Santa Pod, loading all the chrome-moly tube into my truck I would need to build Scott his own junior dragster. A junior dragster I would no doubt be parking next to all the band-wagons we'd jumped on in the last few years…

Around the same time, Maurice bought a vintage dragster of his own, a supercharged, fuel injected, and alcohol burning four-cylinder 'A' Series BMC powered dragster. Called 'Spirit', it was originally built in 1973 and capable of ten second runs. I agreed to go through the car with him and get it prepared while storing it

Scott in his junior dragster

Photo: Jon Spoard

70

in my own workshop. I modified the race-truck to be able to carry not only my dragster, but also Scott's and Maurice's if necessary.

By the start of the 2014 season, Scott's car was complete, and powered by a less conventional (than the more usual Briggs and Stratton), Honda engine for the Junior Stock category. Later when Scott was older this would be upgraded to a purpose-made alcohol fuelled engine based on a Briggs motor.

*   *   *

Along with my injured feet, a broken half-shaft in the Altered followed by a substantial engine blow-up, meant that Rough Diamond wasn't consistently at the track. And then towards the latter half of 2014 I got an out of the blue 'phone call from the highly-respected engine builder Rob Loaring.

Rob had seen a comment on Facebook I'd made about the Nostalgia Funny Car on which he was crew chief at the time, and it reminded him that I knew a bit about running a nitro burning car, and he also considered that I was pretty good at preparing a race car. It transpired that fellow racer Bob Glassup had been putting together all the parts to build a Ford Capri bodied Fuel Funny Car to race in the fledgling Nostalgia category; this class grew out of the desire to run Funny Cars like 'back in the old days' and based on the same sort of nitro powered car I'd been used to working on in the USA. He needed someone to complete the build and run the car for him. Bob and I didn't know each other and our paths had never crossed, but we were aware of each other having been involved in the sport for pretty much the same amount of time. We met briefly at Santa Pod and after a chat on the phone a deal was struck.

Soon after, Alli and I found ourselves in Bridgewater in Somerset filling the back of our Jeep with most of the components Bob had acquired to build the engine and transmission for his Funny Car. Later, he would bring the chassis to me while his friend Richard Walters prepared the Capri body.

Putting together a Funny Car is not a simple task, nor is it for the faint-hearted or anyone who doesn't know what they're doing. Nitro burning engines are dangerous things - it's not a case of 'if' it will go bang, but 'when'. The job of the tuner is to put this off for as long as possible, and with meticulous preparation and a proper maintenance routine, minimize the inevitable damage caused on every run.

Like 'Trigger's Broom', the chassis Bob already had for the task had been around for a long time, and suffered many modifications and changes for whichever class it was going to run in. Much of the works were not really up to a standard I would have liked, and some of the controls were simply in the wrong place. And while Bob was not short of a few bob (no pun intended!), this was clearly going to be, by comparison, a 'low budget' nitro race car (not that any budget for nitro vehicle could be described as low), and he was never going to stump up for a new frame. Ultimately, that would have been better in the long run, but that's what I had to work with.

I built the engine, installed it and the transmission into the chassis, and prepared all the spares, tools and equipment needed to run a six-second nitro burning Funny Car. In June 2015 with Rob Loaring overseeing the procedure, we fired the

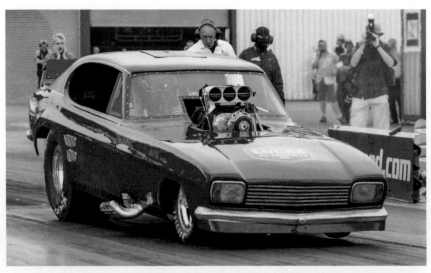

Bob Glassup's 'Bubblegum' Ford Capri Nostalgia Funny Car. I'm standing behind trying to stop his hearing from getting any worse

Photo: Ivan Sansom

72

car up for the first time at my house. A month later we were at Dragstalgia at Santa Pod for the first shake-down runs.

Bob assembled a group of family and friends to work as crew, and I was crew-chief. It was a successful first outing and I went on to run the car for Bob several meetings, each time creeping up on the tune and managing to avoid any real damage.

I was very proud of what we had achieved, and it was great to be working again on a 'fuel' motor, very similar to the ones I'd been working on in 1985 in the USA with Jim Head.

At the end of 2016, Bob came to visit and took us out to lunch, telling me that due to business commitments he wasn't going to continue running the car for the moment. I was disappointed, but at least it meant that I'd be able to run my car again, and keep a closer eye on Scott and Maurice in their cars.

Then in early 2017 my attention was drawn on social media to images of crew preparing the very same car. I called Bob and asked him what was going on, and he told me that he had indeed had a change of heart, and that my services were no longer required.

I was extremely disappointed. I felt that I'd done all the leg work, prepared a plan for Bob to move forward, but I wasn't now going to get any of the glory. They were all good people, but it was poorly-handled. I bear no grudges, but it was hellishly disappointing.

I suspected that it was due to me not being an intrinsic part of his 'racing family' with whom he'd been racing for years. Plus, I was being paid for my time, which I imagine left a sour taste in the mouths of all those that were working on the car at the track for free. I had, of course, been charging Bob for my time to assemble the car in my workshop, and I saw no reason why I should then work at the track for nothing. One thing's for sure, the car would never have got to the track without my input.

I'd assembled a Nostalgia Top Fuel Funny Car, called the shots on the build, and been a Top Fuel crew-chief for a couple of years. Anything else I now did in drag racing would be a step backwards, and the way this ended left a sour taste in the mouth.

Something I've learned in life - know your worth.

*   *   *

I ran the Altered and Scott's car for the next couple of years, I also took the seat of Paul Marston's 'Whoopass' Chevy Monza at the 'No-Prep' events at Rockingham and North Weald. Maurice had a couple of goes in his little dragster, improving all the time, but blowing up his gearbox in the process. The Rough Diamond altered, the Dallara, Scott's junior dragster, and Maurice's dragster all got parked at the end of 2018, and purely for reasons of both time and money, we chose to sit 2019 out.

I'm writing this at the start of 2021 during a global pandemic, so 2020 was also lost to us. I've made some modifications and upgrades to the Altered, and Scott is now too tall to drive his junior dragster, and while he will be old enough this year to drive the Altered - he's too tall for that too!

Right now, I'm not sure what the future holds for us as a family motorsport wise. Both the Dallara and dragster are 'unfinished business', but at this time I don't see a future where we will be racing either of them with any regularity.

Perhaps it's time for a new adventure? Who knows?!

6

Beating time

I was twenty years old, and working with my dad in our tool hire shop. On leaving school, I worked here full time. I have to say I pretty much ran the place on my own, as Dad would spend most afternoons at his brothers' engineering factory not far away in Mitcham.

As previously mentioned, Dad formed 'Gibbons Brothers Engineering' with Jack and Frank, and in an effort to expand into something different they started 'G.B. Tools Plant Hire' which was located in Railway Approach, Wallington. After Jack and Frank decided that they no longer wanted to be in the tool hire business, Dad went on his own. This split coincided pretty much with the earliest opportunity that I could leave school – at fifteen - so it was clear where my future lay – whether I liked it or not, as Dad couldn't run the shop on his own, and nor could he afford to pay a grown man a living wage. I, on the other hand, worked for a roof over my head, food, and a fiver a week.

Across the road from G.B. Tools, on the corner of Manor Road and Melbourne Road, was an early supermarket in the nature of the 'International Stores'. It was not a large store – certainly by today's standards - but it stocked pretty much everything in the way of groceries. Being less than one hundred paces away, in clear view from our shop and across a zebra crossing, I was a regular visitor. I would purchase tea, coffee, and milk on a regular basis, and was known to all the staff. One of the check-out ladies took a shine to me, and it became apparent that she had an ulterior motive, in that she was embarking on a match-making endeavour.

'I wonder Dave,' she enquired, 'whether you might be interested in meeting my daughter? I think you'll have a lot in common. She's very keen on cars.'

At this point one might consider whether to look a gift horse in the mouth or not, so I didn't.

'Yeah, send her over to the shop.'

I offered this response not really expecting anything further, besides, how desperate must she be to have her Mum operating as a match-maker?!

Our shop wasn't large, but we possessed a good-sized forecourt on which we displayed some of the larger pieces of equipment for hire, occasionally there would be a car we were working on. Much of our time was spent just outside the shop door on stools, watching the world go by while drinking tea – often with regular customers or friends. It was not the most attractive of sights.

The next day, I was in my usual spot by the door with tea in hand, when without any further warning, a young lady with a purpose approached me.

'Dave? My Mum sent me over.'

Jackpot.

Karen was five foot two, blonde, and frankly, a pair of boobs on legs.

I was twenty, I'd had a couple of girlfriends, but I'd been educated (and I use that term loosely), at an all-boys' school. So my exposure to the fairer gender had been limited to spending some time with my female cousins, and the daughter of a close friend of my parents. I really hadn't any notion as to how to engage a girl in conversation, they were a mystery to match the meaning of life itself. Armed with an almost complete lack of female experience, having worked with my dad since leaving school, and with Mum running the café next door to the hire shop, most of my 'courting' was carried out in full view of my parents. Not ideal. This perky young thing however, thanks to her mum, was making the task of asking a girl on a date a little less daunting.

If you know me now you may be surprised to discover that at this early stage of my life I was actually shit-scared at the thought of asking a girl out, or rather I was shit- scared at the idea of rejection - it would be different in later years.

Karen lived not far away in a corner house in Demesne Road. Her dad drove a Moskvitch, a car built in the Soviet Bloc, which in the eyes of me and my mate Dick, clearly made him a Communist, because surely only a Communist would buy a Russian car! – I'll be clear though, he wasn't! Her Mum drove an HA Vauxhall Viva which was soon to become Karen's first car as she was about to turn eighteen. At the time I drove a 1963 FB Vauxhall Victor Deluxe, a family car with a column gear change and a bench seat. The beauty of the column-change and bench seat combo, along with the lack of seatbelts, made it a car you could drive with your latest squeeze snuggled up close to you. Fondling on the move wasn't uncommon.

Karen's Mum was correct in her daughter's interest in cars, she enjoyed going to the stock car racing and speedway, so our first date was to Wimbledon Stock Car track. A further date was to 'The Grapes' in Sutton, which had once been was a pub, but was now converted to a Berni Inn - a well-known range of family steak restaurants, serving such delights as prawn cocktail, gammon, egg and chips and Black Forest gateau. The two of us went with Dick and his then girlfriend Sandy, and Dick's cousin Paul the aforementioned 'Spunky'.

In all the years I knew him, Spunky never had a partner, he lived in North Harrow, but spent pretty much every weekend at Dick's. This was a common combination of friends for a night out, and those that were drinking drank, including Karen, who in a fit of giggles splashed her wine all over herself. From then on, thanks to Sandy, she became known to us as 'Tee Hee, Splash Splash' or 'Splash Splash' for short. Karen never knew that. If you are reading this Karen – apologies!

Karen worked at Orton's butchers in Wallington High Street and part time at the International Stores with her mum. Her eighteenth birthday soon arrived, and her parents threw her a party at home. Dick, Sandy, Spunky and myself were invited, as was to our surprise, her previous boyfriend, Eddie, who worked with her at the butchers. I was to be allowed to sleep over - in the spare room. Her dad was having no nonsense under his roof, but little did he know that nonsense most certainly occurred under his roof on a fairly regular basis!

The party wasn't a rowdy do, what with her Mum, Dad and family in attendance, and soon after midnight as the party wound down Dick, Sandy and Spunky went home leaving me there. I popped upstairs to the box room, and Karen came with me to make sure I had everything I needed. We took the opportunity to smooch - as you do. Mid-snog the door flew open, and Eddie was standing there. My, what I thought not unreasonable response to this was to say, 'Oh, piss off Eddie'. It soon became clear that he took exception to this and laid into me with both fists. Did I mention he was a butcher? And he was a big bloke butcher at that. I had little in defence, being only a five foot six, nine stone streak of nothing. The 'Commie' dad was called and he ran upstairs and pulled Eddie off of me. I was pretty well bruised about the face - Eddie didn't have a scratch. It was decided that perhaps I shouldn't stay after all, and as I'd drunk a couple of beers, walked home leaving my car, the FB Victor behind.

That was the one and only time I've been in a fight. Correction, it wasn't a fight - I got beaten up.

The next morning, I woke at home, and Mum and Dad weren't at all impressed when they saw the state of my face. Dad offered to run me back for my car, but I decided to walk, and drove the car off without bothering Karen or her parents. I went to find Dick. I knew he was using a friend's garage that day to spray Sandy's newly acquired Ford Zodiac.

Now, before I met Dick, he'd been in a biker gang, a member of a chapter known as 'The Nightingale'. By this time the gang had disbanded but all remained friends - as they do to this day. It was one of these friends whose garage Dick was using. I can't remember who it was, but they all seemed to have appropriate nicknames, like Beef, Wolf, Ape, and Tiny (who contrary to expectations was actually a small bloke - smaller than me) and Dick was known as… Dick.

I found the garage in Thornton Heath, it was full of purple spray paint fumes, and the state of my face was pretty clear to all.

Having regaled the story of what happened all agreed that Eddie was a 'pussy' for waiting until after my mates had left the party, and an offer from the former Nightingale was made to go and 'sort the bastard out'. Generous though the offer was, I suggested that it probably wasn't a good idea if I wanted to continue a relationship with Splash Splash.

Karen and I continued to date each other, it lasted for a little short of a year. Now to be fair, I was a bit of a prick at the time, and now aged twenty-one there were all sorts of hormones still coursing through my body, and frankly I was a jealous boyfriend. Here I was with a stunner of a girl, and I was convinced that every bloke wanted a piece of the action. With hindsight I should have trusted Karen, but there we are…

In later years, I realised that both my inexperience with the fairer sex, due in part to my all boys' schooling, and the action of powerful hormones in a male body had a good deal to do with how I behaved with women at that time.

(It's partly for these reasons that I wanted to send Scott to a mixed school in order for him to be comfortable in the presence of girls. Unfortunately, that plan recently came off the rails when the Covid-19 pandemic struck and he became home-schooled at age fifteen - a vital time in his relationship development).

One evening I picked Karen up, and to my surprise she'd changed her hairstyle - her long curly blonde locks had been cut into more manageable 'bob'. Irrationally this angered me - who was I to say what a girl could do with her hair? But as I've previously mentioned, I was a bit of a prick at the time. The evening continued as planned but with me in a mood, and my prickness was to rear its head again at the end of the date.

By this time Dad owned the building next door to the hire shop, and rented out the flat and offices above. Dad asked me to collect something from Mike, one of the office tenants, whose habit it was to work from the early evening into the night. (Someone who by the way, I remain in contact with to this day). Leaving Karen outside in the car, I popped up to the office to carry out the said duty. Mike was there with John - a mutual friend, and conversation got around to my girlfriend. Mike also operated from a shop over the road, and John told the tale of how my girlfriend had been in that shop sharing her 'favours' to those in the back room and displaying 'her wares'.

For some reason I chose to believe this story, went back to the car and drove Karen the short distance home, at speed, while shouting at her. Of course, she denied everything, the prick in me choosing to believe the tale of some friends rather than the girl with whom I shared affection!

I pretty much threw her out of the car and drove home - again at speed. I never saw Karen again. It was as if she vanished from the face of the earth. About forty years later Karen's name popped above the Facebook parapet - and we made contact. It transpired that John and Mike told me the story as a joke, and to be fair it's the sort of joke John would play - not realising the implications such a 'joke' may have. Needless to say, I apologised profusely and threw myself upon her mercy - I hope it was accepted.

I'd been a proper idiot. But not for the first or last time over a woman. I have since found myself over the years apologising to ex-girlfriends on a regular basis….

7

The Dating Game

On a couple of occasions my Mum told me that she thought I'd inherited 'the Gibbons curse'. The story was that all of the men in the Gibbons family had 'a weakness for a pretty girl'. Certainly my Dad and his brothers did, and whether this had been handed down a generation, or if it affected any of my cousins I wasn't at the time sure. Speaking only for myself, I had the weakness. Dad always preferred the company of women, as do I, and I've never been one for going out with the lads and getting drunk, or spending time doing 'man stuff', so I guess I inherited this from my father.

Certainly, my uncle John was so afflicted, as he took up with a woman who was not his wife, in fact it was the waitress Mum employed in The Saladin. Once discovered, the affair resulted in an instant divorce between him and my aunt.

As for my parents however, there were times I detected a coldness between Mum and Dad. Many years later I became aware that my father certainly 'fished in someone else's waters'. Have I ever been indiscreet? I am ashamed to say that I have, but that's not for the pages here.

*　　　*　　　*

It was 1974, I was seventeen and working with Dad in the hire shop, and we'd already built my first dragster using a second-hand rolling chassis fitted with a 2.5 litre Daimler engine that we'd pulled from an old car in Curley's breakers yard.

I passed my driving test the first time, having had lessons in an instructor's 1275cc Mini Clubman and practiced my driving skills with Dad in something at the other end of the vehicle size scale - a 1964 Chevrolet Impala. The first car of my own was an automatic convertible 1964 Hillman Super Minx that Dad bought for me. It ran, but didn't actually go along, and if I wanted to drive it I needed to repair it first. Fortunately, the fault was swiftly found - the four bolts holding the torque converter to the flex-plate had sheared, and while it was tricky to get the remnants of the broken bolts out, it was a cheap and quick fix.

Of course, this opened up a whole new world of freedom for me as it does for any youngster who has just passed his test. Prior to this, I got about on a moped, like nearly every other sixteen-year-old, and yes, we terrorised various neighbourhoods on a variety of machinery. A favourite at the time was the NSU Quickly which I owned, as did a friend. I moved on to a Honda and another good friend had been given a new Yamaha FS1E for his birthday - also known as a 'Fizzy'. This clearly made him a God in our eyes and irresistible to the opposite sex.

As I explained earlier, having attended an all-boys' school neither I or my mates had much experience with the ladies, and while having transport was a bonus and got us to places, it was clear that a car was the required form of transport.

I recall being invited to a village disco in Tadworth, which was a pretty long trek - at night - on an NSU Quickly. I managed to engage a rather delightful young lady in conversation and all seemed to be going well - then she found out I was on a moped. In a blink of an eye the music changed and she told me, 'I like this song and I'm going to dance to it, I'll be right back'. *Down on Jollity Farm* by The Bonzo Dog Doo-Dah Band was playing, which is by no means a dance tune – and she didn't come back

I took this as a sign.

So, with Hillman Super Minx on the road, there would be no stopping me now. I had a very innocent relationship with an old school friend's younger sister which was never going to go anywhere, but I thought I was the bee's knees picking her up from school with the top down and the cassette player blaring loudly, I think she may have enjoyed the attention too – even though she lived only a couple of hundred yards from the school.

Dad and I had a good sideline going at the hire shop trading 'old motors.' Generally he'd bag a bargain and I'd 'polish in' some profit. It's amazing how much value can be added with a thorough clean and fitting shiny new number plates and hubcaps. So, I could be driving all sorts of cars at any one time and no-one really knew what I might turn up in - fortunately insurance wasn't the expensive issue that it is these days. One young lady wasn't too impressed with the 1938 Morris Eight I arrived in for sure, so that relationship didn't last too long. I blame it on the car.

(As an aside on the Morris Eight, the hire shop was just over the road from American Autoparts, and with our interest in drag racing and American cars we were on great terms with them and many of their friends too. One such person was John Dodds, who built a faux Rolls-Royce fitted with a Merlin Spitfire engine (the only thing Rolls-Royce about it was the engine and the grille - legal battles ensued). This car had the reputation of being the fastest and most powerful road car ever built, and all sorts of claims were made for its performance - but none of them really stood up to scrutiny. Anyway, we'd bought a car from John and he delivered it to our shop - I was to run him back to Epsom. So here I was with the owner, builder and driver of (apparently) the most powerful car in the world, literally rubbing shoulders with me in the tiny confines of the Morris Eight - and I asked him to operate the choke for the first few minutes of the journey. I'm not sure how he felt about the journey, but it tickled me).

After the Hillman I upgraded - if that's the correct word - to a 1956 Volkswagen Beetle, and dated a Scottish lass for a while - Fiona. Her parents were very religious and they were heavily involved with the Salvation Army, she even played trumpet in the 'Sally Ann' band. I was invited round to meet the parents, however I managed to blaspheme pretty much straight away, which did little to assure them I was the right sort of chap for their girl.

One day I was chatting to her on the opposite side of the approach to the shop, when John Eve (who occasionally helped out in the shop), walked up and down the street shaking a jar of loose change while waving a copy of the Exchange and Mart in his other hand, shouting 'Warcry, Warcry'[9]. I think the humour was lost on her, but everyone else fell about.

---

[9] In those days the Salvation Army used to offer their magazine Warcry on street corners and in pubs in return for a donation to the cause.

I don't believe that had anything to do with the end of that relationship, but a little while after we parted she sent a friend round to my house to deliver a copy of Del Shannon's 'Dream Lover', which is a song in her record collection that I mentioned I liked. Listening to the words of the song years later, I now realize that this may have been an olive branch of reconciliation, but at the time I ignored it. Have I mentioned that I'm an idiot when it comes to girls?

A 1963 Vauxhall PA Cresta came next. I bought it from Paddy Beurke, one of the 'panel beaters' in Forsdick's yard (and the one who taught me to spray cars). Its bodywork was in lilac haze and dusk rose - or two-tone pink to you and me, and I paid thirty-five quid for it. It was in this car that I dated my first 'serious' girlfriend, and if it wasn't for the same car I wouldn't have met my lifelong friend, Dick Hogben. More of him elsewhere.

Debbie was the girl in question, I met her as a friend of a friend, and we even went away on holiday together in that very same PA Cresta - to Leamington Spa. It was the first time either of us had been away from home by ourselves (not including Scout or Brownie camp) and we stayed at the house of one of her relatives – in separate rooms.

I have a feeling that Debbie's mum didn't think I was good enough for her daughter, and that I was possibly a bit below her 'pay grade'. Deb lived in a rather splendid house in Carshalton Beeches - her parents were divorced and she lived with her mum. Her father at the time had a top job with the BBC, and could occasionally be seen giving out sports awards on the telly. He also got us tickets for Wimbledon (but only entrance – not the good seats).

I've alluded to my jealousy elsewhere, helped by the substantial hormones coursing through my nineteen-year-old body. So, this relationship ended, and I have no doubt that it was my fault.

We had a go at reconciliation at a point in time when my parents were on holiday in California. I had the house to myself, and she was planning to stay over. I collected Debbie in the Jaguar XK120 Roadster that we happened to have at the time (it still astounds me that I was driving such a car at that age), and took her home. Unfortunately, her mum had got wind of this plan and followed us. She pulled into the driveway behind the Jag, dragged Debbie from the car and gave me several pieces of her mind. At the time I thought she was being unreasonable, but with hindsight…

That was the last I saw of Debbie for several years, until we were both at the wedding of the mutual friend who introduced us. I was now about twenty-seven and she was married - we pretty much spent the whole evening talking to no-one else but each other.

*　　　*　　　*

One girl who had a lasting impact on me for one very specific reason, was Janet. We met through mutual friends and she lived nearby, I was twenty and she was seventeen. In those days stretchy fabric jean material hadn't yet been invented, jeans were made of good old cotton and girls liked to wear them tight, in fact some jeans were 'shrink-to-fit', where the owner would wear the jeans in a bath of water to shrink them to their shape, and Janet liked her jeans tight. I recall on several occasions walking into the front room of her parents' house, only to find her lying on the floor with her sister Wendy helping her zip up her jeans with the aid of the hook end of a wooden coat hanger.

One day Dick and I were watching her walk away from the hire shop. 'Looks like two ferrets trying to get out of a sack,' said Dick. Janet was known as 'Ferrets' from that day on. Never told her though. Once again, I have to apologise – Janet, in the unlikely event that you're reading this – I'm sorry!

At the time I was driving a variety of cars that were going through our hands, a 1970 Chevy Monte Carlo (with the desirable 400ci small block engine!), a 1954 Chevrolet Yellow Cab, the Model T hot rod I'd just built, and in particular, a 1961 Ford Country Sedan Station Wagon. This last car had three rows of seats and would carry nine people in comfort - and still have room for luggage.

It was Janet's eighteenth birthday, and she wanted to celebrate with her girlfriends in a restaurant in Chelsea - only she needed to get there and back. So, on that night I played token bloke and chauffeur, and drove Janet to Chelsea with seven of her best friends. It was a noisy journey. Once I'd found the venue I just needed somewhere to park, which at least was possible in Chelsea in those days, but finding a gap big enough for a twenty-foot-long land-yacht was proving difficult. Eventually a gap was spotted in a side street - I backed in and parked, all the time under the close scrutiny of a police officer standing outside a house. It transpired that the house in front of which I was parking belonged to Margaret Thatcher - who was well on her way to becoming Prime Minister at the time.

I can only imagine what he must have thought when I got out of the car accompanied by eight giggling teenage girls! He gave me a wry smile and simply commented 'Have a good evening, sir.'

I don't remember why the relationship ended, but end it did as these things often do, and it was almost certainly my fault - again. A few years passed when out of the blue Janet popped her head around the door of our new hire shop in Hackbridge. She'd spent time travelling, working on a kibbutz among other places, and was now back in the UK. The purpose of the visit was to see if I knew of anyone selling a car so she could get herself about, and as it happens I did, and after having a coffee I sent her on her way to Frank Thumwood's garage in Carshalton.

A couple of weeks later, having purchased a Renault 6 (a truly awful car whose looks had the effect of Medusa) from Frank, she popped by again - ostensibly to thank me for the recommendation. It was clear to me that Janet's penchant for wearing tight trousers hadn't diminished, and during the course of our conversation for some reason she felt obliged to disclose to me that she'd 'Forgotten to put any pants on' that morning - I can only imagine that this was a not so subtle attempt at a come-on (it wouldn't be the first or last time I failed to take a hint). Before leaving, she invited me and Dick to a party at the flat she was sharing with a friend in Norbury.

At the time Dick was living with in a flat in Streatham above the car accessory shop in which he worked, and the girlfriend he had at the time had gone to a family function – so off to the party we went.

I picked Dick up on the way for the short drive from Streatham to Norbury which made me the designated driver. We knew no-one there apart from Janet, and while I was on the soft drinks, Dick was putting away the Budweiser. We entertained ourselves quite successfully - Dick was getting merrier by the can. We had a conversation about whether a young lady wearing pyjama type trousers was wearing knickers, so Dick simply asked her - she was not, and the conversation went no further. A little later when some young bloke was dancing with this lady, Dick tapped him on the shoulder and said 'You do know she's not wearing any knickers?' and walked away. Moments later, the fella's hand slid down to the bum of the knicker-less lady, Dick went back, again tapped him on the shoulder and said, 'Told you so.' It doesn't take much to give us a chuckle.

Dick was getting the worse for wear and we decided it was time to go. I went to tell Janet that I needed to get Dick home, she gave me a big squeeze and whispered in my ear, 'Come back, have a drink - you can stay with me.' This appeared to be a gift horse whose mouth I was looking directly into, and a hint that perhaps this time was a little more obvious.

I said I'd think about it.

I bundled Dick into the car and took him back home to his flat. I helped him back out of the car and leant him against his front door and left him there. He told me later that when he got inside he immediately threw up, leaving the girl who'd come back from her function to deal with the mess. Meanwhile, I turned the car around and with a degree of haste went straight back to Janet's flat.

When the party wound down Janet showed me to her bedroom, however any thoughts of romantic shenanigans soon evaporated. Not only did Janet pass out almost as soon as her head hit the pillow, we were sharing the room with at least six other people kipping on whatever soft furnishing they could find to make themselves comfortable. It was no more than I deserved - I was young and foolish. I woke early and stepped over various comatose bodies to get to the bathroom, I decided I should leave. I roused Janet who dragged herself out of bed. I said goodbye, we kissed, and I left. That was the last I ever saw or heard from Janet.

So what was the lasting impact Janet had on me? It was she who suggested I grow a moustache, a moustache that has only been shaved off twice since then. It's almost become my trademark and for that I'm rather grateful. Although it has been said by some, that if they had a nose like mine - they wouldn't underline it...

*   *   *

I'd not long returned from my time in the USA when Peter Hemmings asked me to rebuild a Ford differential for him. Not then having a workshop of my own, I worked in his workshop in Streatham. I came to need a bearing removed and replaced and without having a suitable press on site I went to Sutton Rebore in Lind Road Sutton. Dad had been using these machine shop services since the mid-sixties, and I was well known to them.

On my way to leave I stopped outside to chat with Peter Billinton, a boffin who was instrumental in the creation of Santa Pod Raceway, and indeed built and installed the electronic timing equipment there. As I'd just returned from working on an American Top Fuel Funny Car team we had a lot to talk about, when I noticed a striking young lady walking along the street just over the road. Dark short hair, a brown strappy silk top, and a short white satin skirt.

She noticed the two of us talking, stopped, waved enthusiastically, and shouted 'Hi!'

I looked at Peter, and Peter looked at me.

She then proceeded to trot across the road towards us as fast as her white high heeled strappy sandals would allow - there was jiggling.

'Who's she?' I said to Pete.

'Nothing to do with me.'

She arrived in front of us with twinkling dark eyes and a broad, gleaming smile.

'Dave.'

She knew my name..!

'Yes?'

My bemusement must have been obvious so she continued, 'Lois, Lois G…'.

The penny dropped.

'Fuck!' I said, 'Seriously? You must have been ten when I last saw you!'

Clearly, she was no longer ten years old.

'I'll leave you to it…' said Pete, and walked back into Sutton Rebore.

Her Mum Pam was a friend of Dad's. I have no idea how they knew each other, but I do remember though that Pam worked as an office cleaner. She, with her husband Maurice, had two kids, Lois and older brother Lawrence - both younger than me. When I was just in my teens, I used to cycle to Pam's house during the school holidays and hang out with her and Lois and Lawrence, I guess they were seven and nine respectively.

To be honest, I don't really know how it started, but occasionally I'd get bored helping Dad in the shop so I used to go to Pam's, and he'd come by later in the day, have a cup of tea with Pam, put my bike in the boot of the car and drive me home. I guess it was like having an unofficial child minder. I'd help Pam make cakes with the kids, and she would feed me if I was hungry. The four of us would play board games too, although I never really had much time for Lois and Lawrence – after all, they were SO much younger than me.

Pam also broadened my horizons, she listened to classical music and was a fan of the 'Big Band' sound; I was too as I played the French horn at school. She even took me to see The Glenn Miller Band (although obviously without Glenn!), at the Fairfield Halls in Croydon - a memorable evening and I felt so grown up.

Pam unexpectedly fell pregnant, and gave birth to a girl, Rachel. Subsequently I'd help look after Rachel when I was there and we'd walk in Beddington Park just over the road. I would never dream of spending time with my own Mum like this! When Rachel was christened, Mum and Dad were made Godparents, and at the time I thought it was odd, as they weren't that close. Soon after, Pam was diagnosed with cancer, and succumbed to it quite quickly. My parents didn't take me to the funeral, and I had never seen any of the family again - until this day in Lind Road.

Lois and I chatted, but I needed to get back to Streatham to finish off the differential I'd been working on. It turned out Lois had nothing to do and decided to come with me, so we jumped into the 'Vette and we got to know each other again on the journey.

Clearly Pete was surprised to see me turn up with a girl in tow - it wasn't the sort of thing you'd expect someone to pick up by chance at a machine shop. It was fair to say that she wasn't dressed appropriately for a garage environment, in fact, she was dressed more like the girls in the calendars hanging on Pete's wall… The workshop environment wasn't ideal for a white skirt either, so she spent the time perched on the front wing of the only clean thing in there - a 308 Ferrari.

We carried on talking while I finished up the job, then I drove Lois back to the flat where she was staying. It was clear that she's had a pretty tough time of it since I'd seen her last and life had been very hard. Having run away from home at fifteen, fending for herself, she'd also just come out of an abusive relationship and was 'sofa surfing' until she could get settled. I'm not a fan of tattoos, but the couple that Lois self-inflicted using a fountain pen should have rung an alarm bell. At least she had a job, working at The Eagle Star Insurance Company in Sutton, and soon she moved to another sofa at a friend's house.

We dated, and I'd often (try to), sleep on the sofa with her. Until that is she got a single bed for the spare room - which was marginally more comfortable. This was never going to be a long-term relationship. Unusually for me, I felt uncomfortable around her friends. I also had hopes of getting back together with Paula, who I'd unceremoniously left behind when I went to America. Reluctantly setting aside her eagerness to bestow her favours upon me, I decided to call it a day with Lois.

I bravely wrote a letter setting it out and popped it through the letterbox while she was at work. What an idiot. Unsurprisingly, I never saw or heard from Lois again.

8

It had to be you

It was 1979 and spending my time daily working at G.B. Tools, and our spot in Railway Approach was ideal for people watching as the general public made their way to and from the station. One day I noticed a really cute young thing go by dressed for sport and carrying what was clearly a hockey kit. So with a degree of what might be known as cheekiness, I called out 'Have a good game!' I detected a slight but distinct upturning of the nose and she continued on her way.

The following week she again came by the shop, and again with hockey kit in tow. 'Have a good game!' I called. She stopped, turned, looked me dead in the eye and said, 'The last time you said that, this happened'. She raised her head slightly and indicated to her chin - it sported the most enormous bruise. That was the day I met the woman who would become my wife. I can't remember what I said, it's even possible that I laughed, but I think I had an inkling then that she was 'the one'. We struck up a friendship that lasts to this day.

After a few encounters and chats, Allison (Alli, two ls, Simson no p), agreed to allow me to take her out, but it hadn't quite dawned on me that she was only fourteen years old. Closer to fifteen than thirteen, but I'm sure that didn't make a lot of difference in her eyes, and quite how she got the whole thing past her parents was a mystery. I imagine that the idea of their fourteen-year-old daughter going out with a man who had fifty percent more years to him than her was somewhat difficult to accept - especially one who was tooling about in flashy American cars (I think it was a 1974 Oldsmobile Cutlass at the time). That said, I can't remember when she admitted to me that she was only fourteen. Probably when we were in the pub…

We went out a few times, it wasn't regular, but we always kept in touch. Alli lived a couple of streets away from the shop and would pop in the shop when passing and we'd chat. I know that every time I saw her my heart skipped a beat. As soon as she passed her driving test she picked me up in her Ford Escort and took me out for a drink. I distinctly remember that Mum wasn't at all impressed with the length of (or lack of otherwise), her dress that evening.

Alli took an engineering degree at Portsmouth, during which she took a six month placement in St. Etienne in France. Whenever she was back in Wallington she would come by for a catch up, and again we'd occasionally go out with each other. These days perhaps it might be called a 'friends with benefits' relationship. The years went by, we both dated other people and got on with our lives and simply stayed in touch.

*   *   *

It got to 1987, I'd been back from America for a couple of years, had several failed relationships (did I mention I was an idiot?). I'd reconciled with Paula who I'd dated before going to the States, and was living with her in a flat we were buying together - just around the corner from my Mum and Dad in Carshalton. I'd also started Metmaster so was running my own engineering business.

I can't recall the build up to it, but one evening I was sitting next to Paula on the sofa and said, 'This isn't working is it?' 'No, it's not,' came the reply. No big argument, nothing.

The next morning Paula moved back in with her mum, and we went about the painful process of deciding who would buy who out of the flat, and who would get what of our possessions.

The split with Paula had ended up being fairly acrimonious, followed by something that meant Dick and I wouldn't speak for several years. It transpired that he, my best friend, was now going out with Paula! I can't blame him, I most likely would have done the same, but at the time, quite frankly, I took the news pretty badly.

Several years later, a mutual friend Phil Clark metaphorically banged our heads together, pointing out that Dick and I in the past were great friends and it was a shame that both of us were missing out. He was quite right of course. He arranged a meeting in a pub with some other mutual friends and we both came to our senses. Dick and Paula later got married!!

With a small loan from my parents I managed to keep the flat, but I'd need a lodger to help with making the mortgage payments. You might think that this is where Alli returns - but hold your horses!

I found a lodger, and I also took on an extra job as a delivery driver for a bakery. I'd get up at three in the morning, drive the Corvette to Croydon, load up the bread van and deliver bread, cakes and pastries to various businesses in the area. Usually finishing at around seven in the morning, I'd drive back to Carshalton, grab a cup of tea, and then go to the workshop in Hackbridge and run Metmaster Limited.

To be fair, I was pretty knackered most of the time, but I still managed to play fast and loose, holding parties in the flat and generally being a bachelor.

*   *   *

At this point I should make mention of Sally, if for no other reason than she's likely to read this and ask 'What about me?' So, for her benefit, 'Hello Sally!'

Sally had been on my radar for a number of years. She hung out with a group of kids at a youth theatre club (TWY), including my school friend Clive. Clive went out with, and later married, Sally's older sister. I used to occasionally pop along and support the club's shows and parties, but getting involved never interested me. It's ironic that I ended up working as an actor years later.

Gregarious, outgoing and slim, Sally was taller than me (which always made me feel uncomfortable) and she smoked - which was something I tolerated.

(Both Mum and Dad were smokers, in fact that was the cause of Mum's emphysema, which ultimately was the reason she finally had to stop. Dad smoked cigars - usually Hamlet or Castella - he'd smoked cigarettes previously, and one day when I was fifteen he said, 'If I give up smoking, would you promise never to start?' I agreed.

He threw away his cigars and never smoked again - and I never started. These days fewer people smoke anyway, but I'm always troubled seeing a friend smoking).

Sally liked cars and motorbikes, and we had a really good time together. But in my defence, I had a lot going on at the time.

Then came the great storm of 1987. I don't know what we were up to the night before, but we slept right through it - didn't hear a thing. The biggest natural disaster for over a century in the UK, and it completely passed us by.

The first we knew of it was when I turned the bedroom TV on for the morning news, only to see weatherman John Kettley shuffling himself on a chair - into what looked like a cupboard - to present the weather. Fortunately, apart from a tree falling near the workshop in Hackbridge taking down the 'phone line, we got off scot-free.

Sally was staying over more frequently, and I felt it was getting a little too intense for my liking, and I felt I needed to move on. I ended the relationship - she took it badly.

In recent years I've had the opportunity to apologise, and although she still thinks I was a bastard then, we remain friendly. But to be fair, the height was always going to be an issue - and the smoking.

(On the subject of height, a few years earlier I briefly dated Karin. A girl who was a good five inches taller than me - plus heels! When we held hands, it looked like a Mum taking her toddler for a walk. There was nothing wrong with her – we just looked ridiculous together).

*   *   *

This is where Alli comes back in...

Alli was now in a secure job, and with her parents' help, found a flat to buy in Wallington - almost opposite the fire station, and not too far from her parents. Knowing I owned a van she asked if I'd use it to help pick up some furniture, including a bed. Not a problem - nothing was too much trouble. Getting everything up to the top floor was the worst part of it, and I helped get everything established. (I had a date that night, and somewhat cheekily asked the girl to meet me at Alli's flat! It was a casual, relationship that didn't last).

I was a regular visitor to Alli's home. Along with my Dad's carpentry skills, I helped rip out an old fireplace and install a new one, assisted with decoration, and on occasions it wasn't deemed necessary to go home to my own flat.

Things became exclusive, and both of us had lodgers to help with finances. Sometimes we'd sleep at her flat, on others it would be mine. Over not too much time, my flat seemed to be the preferred accommodation, and after only a few months of property ownership, Alli decided to sell her own flat and move in with me. It made no sense for us to be effectively living with each other with the upkeep of two properties. My lodger stayed on for a while, but when she moved on we had the place to ourselves.

During the latter half of 1988 I decided that I was to propose to Alli, but there were some logistical issues I first needed to get sorted.

*   *   *

Earlier, I mentioned the Crosskeys Youth Club attached to St. Peter's C of E church on the St. Helier Estate. Keith Pound was the curate at the time we were living there, and Dad was one of the people that helped run the club and arrange parish holidays. In fact, Keith attended my christening. Now in his eighties, he remains a good friend.

Over the years Keith worked his way up the clerical ladder, and had a reputation of being a trouble-shooter by going into difficult parishes and establishing the church in the area. He earned the titles 'Right Reverend', 'Archdeacon', and 'Canon', and in 1988 he worked for the Home Office as Chaplain General of the prison service.

As, effectively, our honorary family vicar, I sought his advice. I was fairly confident (if Alli accepted my proposal), a full white wedding was to be expected, but as someone without a religious bone in his body I wasn't about to stand in a church and make promises to a God I knew didn't exist. I sought a suitable alternative.

I visited Keith at the Home Office, and laid out the dilemma. The solution he proposed was for us to have a registry office wedding in the morning, and a church blessing taking the form of a 'normal' wedding in the afternoon. He would write the service to eliminate the religious references that made me uncomfortable. Best of both worlds.

With that sorted, all I had to do was ask the woman to marry me.

*   *   *

November 27th 1988. Why that day I don't know. We'd planned to go to Alli's sister's house in Stevenage for lunch - if it was for a special occasion I can't recall. We were still in bed at 9.45 in the morning and probably should have been getting a move on, and that was the moment I chose.

'Shall we get married?'

'Yes please!'

Very polite, I thought. If it wasn't a special occasion today, it was now!

We decided we'd better pop round to see my parents and tell them before we left.

'Mum, Dad, we've got something to tell you. We're getting married!'

'That's nice,' Mum said, 'What are we doing about Christmas?' That was my Mum all over, get the important things out of the way first.

We enjoyed lunch with my now future sister and brother-in-law, and left a little early so we could visit Alli's parents on the way home and share the news with them - stopping on the way to pick up a bottle of Champagne. Alli's Mum and Dad were (fortunately) delighted, although I think her Dad was a bit miffed that I'd not asked for her hand in the traditional manner.

We picked a date that we felt would give us enough time to arrange everything – 22nd July 1989. Alli agreed that my request to the unusual procedure was the best way forward, so we moved on with the arrangements. All Saints Church in Carshalton was the chosen venue and the resident vicar, Reverend Leigh Edwards, contacted - he invited us in for 'interview'.

Leigh was clearly put out that we didn't want the full standard service - or him - and asked to be contacted by our proposed cleric. The Right Reverend Archdeacon Canon Keith Pound got in touch, and his attitude changed - suddenly he couldn't do enough to make this go smoothly, and the date was booked. However, Reverend Edwards wanted to be sure that we were properly married before the blessing took place.

I should point out that thirty-two years later these things are more flexible, but back then we were pushing the boundaries of acceptability. We needed to book the registry office for the same day with the earliest available slot so we could have the church service we desired.

Registry offices are run by the local council, and the London Borough of Sutton were adamant that we couldn't book a marriage slot more than six months prior - we were nine months away.

So, at 9.30 on the morning on 23rd January 1989 we found ourselves outside the door of Sutton registry office waiting for it to open, we went in and secured the date and slot at ten o'clock in the morning. We also secured The South Hatch Racing Club in Epsom for the reception, a cream and black 1936 25hp Rolls Royce to take us there, and a 1957 convertible Chevy Bel-Air to take us to the hotel in Richmond after. All very appropriate.

We had dreams of honeymooning in St. Lucia, but it soon became apparent that the funds weren't going to be available, so a marginally less glamorous venue, the channel island of Jersey, stepped in as a stand in. Prior to taking the ferry from Poole, we spent two lovely head-spinning days in The Richmond Hill Hotel - the finest hotel in the area.

The family all pitched in, not only assisting with funds, but with dress-making and all the other paraphernalia that goes along with organising a wedding. My old school friend Ian Caple was to be the best man, and Tony Morris would come over from Germany to act as an usher alongside another school friend, Clive Batten. Alli's sister Linda would be maid of honour, and all the family kids agreed to be the wonderful bridesmaids and page boy.

The hen night and stag night went off without incident - such nights weren't as extravagant as they seem to be now, but one chair was broken at the burger restaurant chosen for my stag night - they weren't at all happy about it but my good friend Wug paid for the damage. To be on the safe side, and to make sure I got home, Alli collected me from the restaurant and gave a couple of chums a lift. We got stopped by the police - apparently a young woman driving a Ford XR3 with three fellas on board looked suspicious. When Alli told the police what was going on, they let us go on our way, although one friend in the back of the car had been 'bricking it' as he had a quantity of something in his pocket that he shouldn't have…

The weather forecast was good for the day of the wedding and, as is traditional, Alli stayed with her parents the night before. Tony stayed with me at the flat and was handed the keys to the Corvette to use as his own while he stayed on to visit friends and family for a few days.

Mum and Dad picked me up and took me to the registry office, as did (have I introduced Freddie and Sheila as Alli's parents yet?) Freddie and Sheila with Alli. We were all suited and booted, and Alli wore what was going to be her 'going away' outfit that would come into play later that evening. Our good friend Ron Pudney Jnr. was the only other guest. As a sometime professional photographer (among other things), he was also there to record events. The registrar seemed surprised at the scale of the function, or rather the lack of it. We really were treating it as 'getting the paperwork done'.

At the end of the morning I met some friends for a drink in the nearby Greyhound pub and took the short walk to the church. But by Christ it was getting warm! I was greeted by Keith who was wearing his newly acquired robes and cassock, newly acquired, because unbeknown to us he'd recently been appointed The Queen's Honorary Personal Chaplain! And he was damn well going to wear the robes that went with the job!

Myself, Alli and Keith Pound

But my word was it hot. Inside the church everyone was roasting. Alli was slightly late (delayed, as brides always tend to be, by the photographer), and she looked perfect as she entered the door at the rear of the church. Apart from going into the vestry to sign the register, this was to all intents and purposes a normal wedding.

The two of us stood in front of Keith, the three of us sweating profusely (or in Alli's case 'glowing'). I watched as perspiration ran down Keith's nose, collected at the tip, and dripped regularly onto his script.

Everything went to plan. The photos were taken outside in the park by the ponds opposite the church. It had been a hot summer so far, and it continued on this day. The grass and the shrubs were beginning to turn brown, and our guests did what they could to remain looking smart while trying to remain cool - which was impossible.

The Rolls took us to the South Hatch Club for the reception. It wasn't a large venue and we had to restrict the numbers for the 'sit down' meal, but the speeches went well. I managed to bring several guests to tears - and had them laughing too. Alli's Dad Freddie made a crack about having Keith there being like 'Bringing your own ref to a rugby match', and Ian read out the 'telegrams' inserting one of his own. 'This is from Richard Brown, I hired a lawn mower from you in 1983 and I still can't get it started!'

There was a limit imposed by the venue on numbers of guests in the evening which we clearly ignored, and as the 'float' put over the bar ran out, my dad added some more. The '57 Chevy arrived with its top down and looking fabulous to take us to the hotel, the location of which was a closely-guarded secret. Alli hadn't yet changed into her going away outfit and decided not to bother, so still in her wedding dress we climbed into the back of the Chevy with a plan for Alli to throw her corsage from the back of the car into the crowd as we drove off. It started to rain. The owner of the Chevy was insistent that he raise the roof in order to keep his pristine upholstery dry, and to an extent I can't blame him, so the flowers were tossed out of the open window instead. But that, if anything, was the only disappointment of the day.

The journey seemed to take forever, and it became quite clear that the driver was lost, but with some guidance from the back seat we got there eventually. The Richmond Hill Hotel and its guests were treated to the sight of Alli in full wedding garb arriving at the reception desk, and they treated us like royalty.

We spent two days in Richmond before driving to Poole (we'd left the XR3 in Richmond with our packed bags the day before the wedding). Planning to hire a car in Jersey, we parked the Escort in the long-term car park and boarded the ferry to Jersey. Staying at the Hotel De France we were greeted warmly, we were shown to our room, 413. It wasn't a very nice room at all, with a view of nothing but the heating plant at the rear. Nor was there any sign of the 'complimentary Champagne wedding package'.

Alli unpacked our bags while I returned to reception in search of the Champagne. I was told that it was definitely there - I told them it definitely was not! The receptionist came with me back to the room to check, and only then the error was uncovered. The bell-boy heard 'Room 413' when it was actually Room 430! Assisted with our belongings from one room to another we found ourselves in a delightful (much bigger) room (complete with now warm Champagne), overlooking the hotel entrance, its swimming pool, and the rest of Jersey beyond. Aside from that irritant, the remainder of the honeymoon was a wonderful break in glorious weather in a lovely place. Not St. Lucia by any stretch of the imagination, but splendid nonetheless.

On arrival back at Poole we found not a trace of our Escort XR3 in the car park, and of course feared the worst - such cars had a reputation for being stolen. We went to security to be told they 'secured' our car as, in fact, an attempt had been made to steal it. So they made it safe as a rear side window had been smashed to gain entry - fortunately there was no further damage and they got no further. My first job on arriving back at Carshalton was to have the window replaced. Bloody nuisance.

*   *   *

Ian had brought the wedding gifts back to the flat for us, so we looked at all of those, which was lovely. There was also the pile of post that had built up while we were away. Among the letters was one to Alli from her employer - a small engineering company in Surbiton. While we were away they decided to make her redundant - effective immediately. Another letter was from the bank - her last pay cheque had bounced.

I'd left a list of work that needed to be done with my Metmaster manager, using a highlighter pen to indicate the most urgent and important works. On my return and inspecting the list, none of the urgent works had been done. The bloke working for me had never seen the use of a highlighter pen before - and thought I'd crossed them all out…

All in all, it could have been a better return to reality, but you know what they say, when life gives you lemons, pour a glass of vodka. In this case a large one.

It was the beginning of a wonderful journey, and every now and then, my heart still skips a beat.

9

Give me Head 'til I'm dead

From the age of twelve I worked part time for Dad in the hire shop, but for a brief period I had a Saturday paper round - I hated it. It was with the newsagent just along from our shop in Manor Road. Like any paper round, it started earlier in the morning than should be necessary, but I'd go to the back of the shop with my bike and collect the morning's papers. By Christ the bag was heavy! I was only a little fella although quite strong for my size and age, but dragging that bag around the streets of Wallington felt like slave labour. With hindsight I probably could have split the load, but I guess I just did what I was told. I decided I wasn't that desperate for the money and knocked it on the head after about four weeks.

At fifteen, with the school realising that I was going to work with my dad, they washed their hands of me and sent me on my way. Elsewhere in these pages I've mentioned the life experience I accrued in Railway Approach, but I also learnt a lot of practical skills - mostly maintaining tools and equipment. All sorts of skills came into play, mechanical, electrical, even woodwork and painting - I got to be quite a dab-hand at fixing Kango hammers! Of course, customers would also expect advice on how to operate the tools and often how to do the job they were intending to do. Sometimes it was like spinning plates trying to keep everything working - and Dad wouldn't buy a part unless we really needed to!

From very early in my childhood I'd learnt a great deal about internal combustion engines, but here I was learning the basics of welding and fabrication. If and when necessary I'd have the run of my uncle's engineering factory in Mitcham too.

We also bought and sold a good number of cars. I'd spend time 'polishing in the profit' of various motors that came our way ready to move on, repairing and refurbishing as necessary. I also learnt a reasonable amount about automotive body repairs from the ne'er do wells who worked in the lock-ups behind our shop. At this time we also built the first two of my race cars, giving me skills to build upon and remain in use to this very day.

By the time 1980 came around we'd moved to a new location in Hackbridge, and at the rear of the shop was a small workshop, and we rented this out to the upholsterer Peter Jones.

Pete was a bit of a rogue and I think he spent almost as much time in our shop talking bollocks to me and Dad as he did on his upholstery. They had a love of the sea in common, Pete had his Captain's papers and taught Dad navigation, with my old man eventually getting his qualification. I'd also go and help Pete collect larger items of furniture for re-upholstery, which eventually led me to me learning the tricks of the upholstery trade itself. And Pete knew all the tricks.

Occasionally the pair of them would go off for a few days and move small vessels from location to location, this meant that sometimes I not only held the fort for the hire shop, I was also looking after the upholstery side of things too.

Pete also taught upholstery evening class at the Sutton College of Liberal Arts. Dad used to go and assist him, which led my old man talking himself into a job teaching basic car maintenance at evening classes too. It's at this point you might see how the 'getting away with it' thing ran in the family. I went on to assist Dad, and ended up getting a minor teaching qualification of my own.

Then 1985 came around and I got the call that would take me to the USA.

*   *   *

Having applied for the job of crew member on Jim Head's Top Fuel Funny Car team by answering an advert in *National Dragster* magazine, I didn't expect any response at all. However, a letter arrived asking me to telephone Jim directly, which I did. However, to his (and my), annoyance, his secretary posted the letter by surface mail rather than air mail to save on the postage – and it took six weeks to get to me. The job had been taken.

However, after an extensive chat, Jim told me that if one of the two men he'd just taken on didn't work out, he'd give me a call.

I was taken aback when exactly that happened a couple of weeks later. Not as much however as my parents and girlfriend Paula who'd remained blissfully unaware of any of this, so sure I was that it could not possibly ever happen. Jim invited me out on a trial basis if I could get myself to Columbia, South Carolina (at my own expense), by the next Friday. On the day that I left Dad sat on the stairs that led down to the kitchen and cried - I'd never seen him cry before.

I was met by Jim Weaver, John Davies and Mark Conyers in the arrivals lounge of Columbia airport the following Thursday night, and taken straight to the hotel where several eighteen-wheeler race trucks were parked up - including Jim's. By that time I was busting for a pee, and was told that perhaps I should 'go' behind one of the trucks. The chosen truck happened to be that of drag racing legend and champion Kenny Bernstein. It seemed ironic, as a few years earlier while at a race in Orange County California, I'd spoken to Kenny and asked what I might have to do to get a job on a race team. On discovering I was from England he assured me that I wouldn't have any chance at all. This made the event that would later occur in Baton Rouge, Louisiana so much sweeter.

Early the following morning we arrived in the truck at the race track, and parked amongst the seemingly endless row of semi-trailer race trucks. While I was being shown around the trailer and having my 'induction' I heard an English voice, 'What the fuck are you doing here?'

I looked over to the adjacent trailer only to see fellow Brit Dave Fletcher standing in the doorway of the John Force trailer. Dave had been involved with UK drag racing almost as long as me, and had joined Force's team the year before!

Initially, I stayed at Jim's house in Columbus Ohio with Mark - Jim was recently divorced and his home was currently redundant. After a couple of weeks, we rented a condominium together, a nice spacious place with a communal pool - not that we got to use it much.

The race workshop was on the property for the head offices of Head Inc., a large construction company that built major government buildings. It was huge by comparison to anything I'd seen before, and well equipped. We could get the Peterbilt semi-truck and trailer in there, but we parked it alongside where it became an extension of the workshop between races.

Both Mark and I were given the use of a pool of cars to get about in, and I have to say we pretty much existed on take-away and drive-through food. The fridge in the workshop was always well stocked with soda (and piss-weak American) beer.

It was bloody hard work - constantly. Days were long, and we rarely had any time off. Jim Head is an innovator, and always wanted to 'build a better mousetrap', experimenting with various things in order to gain a slight advantage. We didn't have the fastest car, but it was one of the most consistent - by that I mean it didn't blow up very often. In those days the nitro cars were much more volatile than they are now, and engine explosions were not only common but expected. Our car wasn't as hard on parts as others, but to go rounds in eliminations we would 'consistency them to death' as Jim would put it.

When we weren't repairing the car, we would be preparing spares - engines, heads, transmissions, clutches and so forth. It was relentless, but it was the same for every team. I saw a lot of America, but only through the window of the Peterbilt.

It was deemed that it would be helpful if I could share some of the truck driving. I had in the past driven Pat Mannion's Revolution Wheels duple coach, which was converted to a transporter for his special saloon race car, but a full-on eighteen-wheel rig with thirteen gears was a whole new experience - and I was thrown in at the deep end. I wasn't quite sure of the legality of me driving this truck on a UK driving licence, but I was assured 'It would be fine'. To be on the safe side I decided to take my Ohio driver's test, plus the optional 'chauffeurs' upgrade so I could legally drive the truck - this part also required a medical.

I studied the six-page pamphlet 'How to pass your driving test', got myself a medical examination, and booked myself in. After having my photo taken my examiner took me into the car park where I drove the firm's Oldsmobile around some cones. I was given a 'multiple guess' form to complete for my car driving licence, and for the 'chauffeur's upgrade' - an additional 'multiple guess' questionnaire. Seriously, all it took to be allowed to legally drive the behemoth that is a tractor and trailer rig on the roads of America, was to fill out a couple of forms. Scary.

I had to answer a 'multiple guess' form in order to legally drive this rig

As you might imagine there was a lot of travelling, we'd try to get to the track in one day but it wasn't always possible, but now with three of us sharing the driving (two in the front - one in the sleeper), meant we stopped for very little. One time I was asleep in the back when I got a prod and heard 'Wake up Dave, it's your turn to drive', only to rub my eyes and see both Weaver and Conyers on the passenger side of the cab with Weaver guiding the truck at fifty-five by holding the wheel steady with his left hand. I dragged myself into the driving seat and decided that I might actually now be awake.

At the races it was a team effort - the five of us all had a job to do and servicing the car between rounds was a joint effort. But back at the workshop between races we had more time, and one thing that made me particularly proud was that I soon became the person that built the engine that would be in the car for the first round of qualifying. While Jim would decide on the ultimate 'tune' that would go in the car, I built a good number of five-second motors, and I don't recall any of them blowing up.

Spinning the wrenches on Jim Head's Funny Car

I soon became nominated 'the warm up monkey' or 'the bloke that sits in the race car while we warm it up'. If you don't know anything about 'fuel' drag racing, it will be hard to comprehend how loud and dangerous these machines are - even when idling in the pits. Nitro-methane fuel is a high explosive liquid, generally safe to handle, but under pressure it becomes highly volatile and unstable, and when used in an internal combustion engine, especially one that is also supercharged, each cylinder has the equivalent of a small bomb going off on every ignition stroke, and if for some reason the ignition doesn't fire it, the quantity of fuel will 'hydraulic' in the cylinder and simply explode. How on earth we are allowed to actually do this stuff remains a mystery to me.

One Sunday during eliminations at Thunder Valley Dragway in Bristol, Tennessee, we'd won the first round and the car was prepared and ready for the next race. Generally we had an hour and a half to service the car between rounds, and when I say service the car, I mean remove the cylinder heads and all of the pistons and con-rods, basically perform a complete engine rebuild, re-fuel the car, re-set the clutch and make a myriad of adjustments and tune up changes, and warm it up and check systems - we could get it all done in an hour if we were lucky.

I took my seat in the car while Jim fired the car up from the outside, initially only on alcohol and then switching the fuel pump on for the nitro. All was fine, and then Jim 'whacked' the throttle (not only is this loud, makes the spectators jump, and is *really* cool, but it also 'sets' the clutch plates). There was a huge bang, a large explosion, and a cloud of smoke and steam. I could see nothing, but grabbed the fuel shut off and hauled on the brakes to get the wheels stopped. When the noise ended and the smoke literally cleared I found myself alone, sitting in the car with not a soul in sight. Gradually, one by one, heads appeared from around the adjacent trailers. The motor had indeed 'hydrauliced', kicking out a head gasket and taking out a chunk of cylinder head. We had to change the entire motor – in thirty minutes…

I sat in the car and guided it as it was being towed to the start line. Mark was standing on one set of exhaust headers while Johnnie was on the other, they were installing the spark plugs and fitting the plug leads as we were moving, while Jim was in the tow car putting on his protective fire-suit and equipment. There was no time to warm up the motor, but we got there just in time to get Jim in the car and fire it up. I'd like to say that we won the race with record setting time and speed, but unfortunately, no. We had no time to make some small adjustments, but while the car ran well, the wheels spun and smoked the tires. We lost.

On some days, especially on a hot day in Atlanta, the work was extremely tough, and I do recall hoping at times that we didn't win the next round so that I wouldn't have to go through all of that again. It hadn't taken long for what was originally my hobby to become bloody hard graft.

One of the illicit T shirts, framed and on the wall of my study

(We sold 'Give me Head till I'm dead' T shirts from the back of the trailer, in fact many of the teams sold merchandise from their rigs to raise a little funding and promote a fan base. Until one day we got a visit from the top brass of the NHRA – the organising body. They were most unhappy that our T shirts didn't reflect the sort of family values they were trying to promote, and ordered us to cease their sale forthwith. Of course we complied, sort of - the remainder got sold off surreptitiously. Subsequently the NHRA ordered that all racers merchandise had to be approved before going on sale. The fact that the logo should read 'til rather than till didn't seem to bother them, but that sort of thing keeps me awake at night).

Baton Rouge in Louisiana will always be one of my favourite places - the race-track was the home of The Cajun Nationals. While Jim had finished in the top ten of the previous year's championship, he was also deemed an underdog by virtue of his privateer status. There were other 'privateers', but everyone else in the top ten was funded substantially.

We qualified the car thirteenth in the sixteen-car field with consistent high five-second passes while all the heavy hitters were running two tenths of a second faster. Jim got lucky in round one where his opponent had problems and shut off, allowing Jim to save his parts for the subsequent runs. As usual, Jim took the 'consistency them to death' approach and won some close match ups, until we found ourselves in the Final.

Our opponent was Kenny Bernstein (whose truck I had peed behind on my arrival), not only one of the best funded drag racers at the time being sponsored by beer giant Budweiser, but also defending champion. Head beat Bernstein off the line, but

Bernstein had problems and Jim won the race with yet another 5.9 second run.

Cajun Nationals winners' circle. In those days it only took five people to run a nitro funny car

So there I was, in the winners' circle, standing next to 'Miss Winston' while Jim accepted his trophy. We packed up, returned to the hotel, cleaned up, and had one hell of a time in the restaurant. Event commentator Steve Evans joined us, and started the food fight, and I had a very drunken phone conversation with my dad when I called to tell him of our success. I was told later that a nineteen-year-old Shelly Anderson (later to become a successful Top Fuel dragster racer and daughter of Top Alcohol drag racer Brad), had been apparently flirting with me. I was too drunk to notice...

The following morning at breakfast we were treated to a constant flow of legendary drag racers coming to our table to congratulate us. I was particularly struck by Gary Beck, the first drag racer in the fives, who was genuinely warm, and full of praise to each of us in turn.

While working for Jim I got to know a lot of the most famous people in drag racing, people I'd been reading about for years. Don Prudhomme, possibly the next most famous drag racer in the world after Don Garlits, once asked to borrow a broom from me. Which is a bit like being a football fan and having Ronaldo ask to use your phone!

It also became clear that opportunities were opening up elsewhere if I wished to take advantage, including Frank Hawley who was setting up his race school at the time. The idea of working on race cars and not having to travel was quite appealing.

I was on first name terms with some of the most respected names in the sport, one in particular was Joe Pisano - the stocky Italian-American seemed to take a shine to me, he loved the fact that I was English. Joe not only ran his own race cars, but manufactured major engine parts like pistons and connecting rods. At the time Keith Black made the weapon of choice when it came to engine blocks, but Joe came up with an improved design of his own version of the Chrysler 'Hemi' motor - the JP1.

Joe and Jim were good friends, and Jim got the third JP1 block out of the machine shop, and handed it to me to assemble. I found an oil way had not been completely drilled through - if the motor had been started it would have been disastrous. Spotting this fault saved a lot of grief for Pisano, and he was complimentary of my meticulous attention to detail. I got a lot of ribbing from Weaver about my 'friendship' with Joe Pisano. There was also suspicion that Joe might have been 'connected' due to his Italian heritage. I doubt very much that was true, but there was always a lot of money floating about the sport - and Jim, along with others, was ready to splash it about.

(During a rainstorm I saw several of the leading racers in the country, including Jim, playing poker in the back of one trailer, there was an inordinate amount of cash on the table. At another event, Jim decided to buy everyone pizza, and gave someone $1,000 in cash and sent him out with instructions to blow it all on pizza. Quite what the local Pizza Hut made of that I don't know, but the guy returned with a LOT of pizza!

Top Alcohol racer Dennis Forcelle - another friend of the team - ran a company supplying the solid copper head gaskets that most of the racers used at the time. On Dennis' birthday, Jim paid for a plane to fly above the track towing a 'Happy birthday Dennis, love Jim' banner behind it. It was extravagance I wasn't used to. The scale of money was alien to me).

Another man I got to know quite well was Scott Kalitta, whose Dad Connie was and remains to this day, a legend of drag racing. He'd been racing Top Fuel in one way or another pretty much since the early sixties, and was a force of nature in his own right. Alongside running successful Top Fuel dragsters, he established a hugely successful air freight business. Today he owns over fifty 747 cargo planes.

Scott was a little bit younger than me and was driving the 'Bounty Hunter' Top Fuel Funny Car for Connie, and I got to know him pretty well - most of the racers were in and out of each other's pits either buying or borrowing parts from each other, and Jim was particularly generous in this way.

One day we were at the Englishtown track in New Jersey, which, due to local bylaws, is a 'dry' track - meaning no alcohol was allowed on the venue. The Jim Head team smuggled some in, and Scott got wind of the fact that I had access to beer and was begging me for a twelve pack. I told him I'd swap it for one of his Bounty Hunter tee shirts and the illicit deal was done. Sadly, in 2008, Scott was taken from us in a horrendous 300-mile-per-hour crash at New Bridge Township raceway in New Jersey, which was to have lasting implications for the sport. In an attempt to reduce top speeds, the sanctioning body shortened the length of the track for Top Fuel drag racing to one thousand feet from the traditional quarter-mile. The tee shirt remains a treasured possession.

Jim was busy playing at being bachelor again, using the 'I'm a multi-millionaire' ploy, occasionally combined with the 'by the way I also drive a 250mph race car' chat up line. He soon added pilot to that list too. Now while I'm sure he intended it to be a privilege for me, I got rather fed up with ferrying his girlfriends about. On one occasion when we were in Montreal, he asked me to collect his current squeeze from the airport, albeit I was to do so in the new Z28 Chevrolet Camaro that he'd rented for the weekend.

This meant I was not there for some of the prep work at the track, and I somehow felt that I clearly wasn't needed there - my role was insignificant. Looking back, I'm sure that's not the case, but that was the way it appeared, and that was how I felt about it.

Throw in the fact that as I was there on a visitor visa I was effectively an illegal alien (Mark would frequently sing the tune 'An Englishman in New York' by Sting, swapping out the word 'legal' for 'illegal') and while we did make efforts to 'legalise' me, they were proving difficult, expensive, and came to nothing. The fragility of the situation was brought home when we were on the way back from Montreal - we had concerns that returning across the Canadian border in a 'working' truck wearing team uniform - perhaps I'd be 'tumbled' and sent home.

It was a good life, and although well rewarded with great perks, having been away for much of the year I really was missing home. Mum, Dad, my friends, and the girl I'd left behind. Yes, I was making friends in the USA, but it was all a bit 'hollow'. And being relegated to being Jim's girlfriend's driver, I wasn't really feeling valued as a team member. So, I pulled the plug and decided to come back to the UK. I gave Jim two weeks' notice which took us to the other side of the next race meeting.

I said my goodbyes and got on a plane home.

10

Back with a (bit of) a bump

Somewhat foolishly I'd imagined that when I got back nothing would have changed and I could pick up pretty much where I left off, but things are never that simple. Dad still had the hire shop, but managed to find someone to help look after it, and he'd decided to retire. He was also converting the coach house (that we'd used as a workshop), into a dwelling with the intention of moving into it and selling The Yews. For the time being I was back at home with Mum and Dad, but I needed to work. I worked for whomever I could, and among others, our old friend Pat Mannion stepped in.

Irishman Pat was a builder (which is how we came to know him - he was a customer in the hire shop), who raced cars as a hobby in the sixties. Identifying a need for alloy wheels in motorsport, he created the race wheel company Revolution Wheels. He began by making them in the garage at his home in Wallington, outsourcing the foundry work and carrying out the machine work himself. Later the operation moved to a factory in Hackbridge, but shortly after I'd returned for the USA, he was in the process of moving into a brand-new industrial unit on a trading estate in Beddington.

Some years earlier (while I was racing the Rough Diamond T), Pat approached me with the idea of me heading up an outlet of Revolution Wheels in the USA. It was an enticing idea, but I told him that it would be like 'taking coals to Newcastle' and unlikely to succeed. At the time the dollar exchange rate wasn't favourable and the cost of importing wheels to the USA would not have made it a viable operation. Shame, I quite liked the idea.

Initially I panelled out the inside of his new van, and then I helped prepare the new factory. I sealed the floor of the entire 40,000 square feet, and installed a variety of machinery, and generally did whatever was necessary for the move in - and beyond. I also got to crew for him with his Sunbeam Stiletto Special Saloon which he was racing in the Wendy Wools series.

As the work on Pat's new unit wound down, another old customer of the hire shop, Peter Pitts, came to the fore. Peter owned Pitts Contracting, and sponsored me for some parts for the Topolino version of Rough Diamond. He also bought the Model T hot rod from me that I built when I was twenty-one to keep at his holiday home in Alderney.

He discovered a need for a small engineering service to carry out metalwork for Pitts Contracting, and decided that he'd like to invest in a metalwork service that could do both this, and work for other companies. Peter approached me to run this new venture. To be honest, I was out of my depth as far as the business side of things went but, as they say, 'training will be given'. Initially I was to outsource the bulk of the fabrication work and carry out some of the fitting myself. Peter set me up in an office he owned over the road from his own in Sydenham, invested in a car and a van for me, gave me a list of contacts, put money into an account, and sent me on my way. Thus, Metmaster Limited was created.

Not long after it became apparent that I'd need to change premises. The first I knew of this was when I heard a noise outside my office window. It was a man fitting a 'For sale by auction' board to the building. I queried this with Pete.

'Ah, yes, I knew there was something I meant to tell you.'

Fortunately, Dad came to the rescue once again (it's what good Dads do). He was by now in the process of selling the shop in Hackbridge, but decided to split the property and retain some of the yard and the workshop that was once the 'upholstery department'.

We created within it an office from which to operate Metmaster, and left some of it to use as a (very) small workshop. With further investment from Peter for equipment, I began to employ staff to carry out the on-site works.

I'd like to say it went from strength to strength, but it didn't. Finding reliable staff was a never-ending problem - especially ones with any sort of initiative. All of them were taking home more than I was every week, and I was battling with them making mistakes, forgetting to take the correct equipment with them - and keeping them out of the café. It was soul destroying.

It became apparent that there was a need for me to be contactable. I had no-one to man the office, and my staff needed to be able to contact me when things went awry. We'd managed with pagers for a while, but I needed something more.

Car-phones had been around for a few years, and mobile phones were bulky items that had to be carried like a heavy, unattractive handbag. Then a company called Excell came into being, they produced what they called the first 'pocket phone', but measuring 18 x 8 x 3cm you needed a pretty big pocket, and having one in your pocket made you look deformed. Calls both to and from the phone were charged, and the cost of calls were similar in cost to calls to the USA. It was prudent to advise a caller that they were calling a mobile phone and you would call them back. They also cost £1,800, not to buy, but to lease! Of course - I had one!

Carrying an Excell phone was a bit like having an ingot of gold in your pocket - but worth more. And when using the Excell 'pocket' phone in public people would invariably stare. Perhaps because it was unusual to see a mobile phone at the time, but more likely because you would be shouting at the top of your voice. It was very difficult to have a private conversation.

By now I'd moved into the flat in Beechwood Court with Paula and had a mortgage, so it wasn't like I could just stop running Metmaster. Fortunately, Pete would continue to invest to keep the firm in business, but eventually that dried up and I had no choice but to continue by 'flying solo'.

Metmaster ran for about five years in total, but we were in the midst of a recession and, try as I might, I couldn't get in front. The bank had extended the company a sizable unsecured loan, and really would have liked the money back please, that or put up the flat as security. I wasn't about to do that, as by this time I'd married Alli and she owned half the flat with me - she didn't get me into this mess, so why should she take any of the risk?

I spoke to my accountant, we looked at the books and said to me, 'Just stop, stop now.' I went back to the workshop, gathered the four men I employed together and gave them each two weeks' notice.

Metmaster simply stopped trading. A huge weight was lifted from my shoulders - oh and the mobile phone was re-possessed.

*   *   *

Dad once again stepped up and helped, by investing in the property by paying for an extension to the workshop, a perimeter wall to be put up, and the yard to be concreted over. I worked as a labourer on all of the work, and eventually found myself with a workshop from which I could operate - this time on my own, working on race cars and street rods. Well that was the idea in principle, but I also carried out servicing on people's daily drivers as well. I was also carrying out some general engineering and fabrication work too.

I soon discovered that the problem with working on other people's race cars and 'rods, was that the vehicle would be stuck with me for months on end while waiting for parts, or in the main, payment. And with only space for one car at a time it proved challenging. I stopped working on complete vehicles, choosing only to carry out work that I could 'pick up and put on the bench'.

Although it wasn't that straight forward…

11

I'm not a Star Wars fan but…

At around the time Metmaster folded I'd been sitting waiting in my local hairdressers reading one of the weekly 'gossip' magazines when I saw an article about working as a film extra.

Now at that time, the film business was a 'closed shop' and it was no different for film extras - or walk-on artists. Fortunately, I'd been involved in some film work in the past by virtue of owning cars that had appeared in films and TV, and had connections with both Action Vehicles and Nine-Nine cars, both film industry specialists. I'd even appeared in the film *Mountbatten - the Last Viceroy* as Mountbatten's chauffeur, when I supplied our Rolls-Royce for use in the film. Special dispensation was made as it wasn't possible to find a union extra to fit the role as well as possessing the skill to operate a valuable Rolls.

(The same could not be said when my Corvette was used in an episode of *Dempsey and Makepeace* - they hired an extra who could (apparently), drive a left-hand drive car. It turned out to be a slight untruth, and terrified me when he had a go to 'get to grips' with the car. In the end the 'Vette was never needed to be seen driving anyway).

I 'phoned the Film Artistes Association - the film extras union, requesting details of how to join. Mentioning that I occasionally worked for vehicle suppliers, I was called in for interview.

With my best bullshitting hat on, I attended, named some names involved in the vehicle business, and with my experience with the Rolls and the Corvette, suggested that it might be helpful to be able to be in possession of a union card so I could drive on camera if required. To my surprise the union chief agreed with me, and not only issued me with a card there and then, sent me off to the extras' agency Central Casting with instructions that they should sign me up as a film extra.

It was cold and wet at Shepperton film studios a week later where I was to be a 'villager' in *Robin Hood Prince of Thieves*. It

119

was an early start and they dressed me in what was pretty much sack-cloth, and sent me through makeup to get 'grubbied up'. It was an interesting day while trying to learn the ropes as I went along without wishing to appear as a first-timer. A couple of chickens got accidentally blown up that day, but thankfully it wasn't my fault!

Everyone was paid in cash at the end of the day by the second assistant director. I was handed my £82 and asked to come back tomorrow. I walked away, thought about it for a moment, and decided that I didn't really want to. I was cold, and damp, and the food was rubbish. So, I fought my way to the front of the queue again and told them I'd changed my mind. It didn't go down well. I was soon to discover after that this was how the system worked, once you were on a big film like this, you could pretty much be on it for weeks.

After a while I started 'checking in' with Central Casting more frequently and it worked like this. If you knew you were available to work the following day you would 'phone in the afternoon. If there was nothing that matched your profile there was a 'Not today' response, but if they were expecting something suitable, the reply would be 'Not at the moment' which meant you could try again later in the afternoon. I quickly learnt that the film business is very much a last-minute affair, and casting breakdowns weren't usually sent out until the day before. It was also most often long days and early starts, it was also before the days of Satnav, so it was down to a good old-fashioned A-to-Z map book, and if you were lucky, prior knowledge of the area.

I found myself checking in more and more frequently, and working fairly often. There would be a lot of sitting about, and sometimes I wouldn't get used at all - which was fine, as I still got paid. The FAA union negotiated the fees, and among the standard day, night and overtime rates, there were additional fees for using another set of your own clothing, special skills (like driving, playing a sport), minimal dialogue, and 'special action' with a main character. On a good day the fee could end up being quite substantial.

It quickly became clear to me that there were regulars who had been doing this for a long time, and knew how to 'play the odds' by keeping a low profile in order to be kept on longer, or that there might be some 'special action' in the offing. There were also the favourites, those that were well-known to the assistant directors and would clearly get the bulk of the good stuff.

The key was, as it is in any business, you had to work at it. Be pleasant, don't cause any trouble, do exactly as you are asked, go beyond expectations, and hit your marks. All the while, not being obvious on camera. It was also handy to be able to react well to someone shouting 'bang!'

Gradually I worked my way up the metaphorical extras ladder and got closer to being an 'A team' crowd artiste - or supporting artistes as the serious ones prefer to be called (though frequently known as 'noddies', because we stand in the background and 'nod' to each other while pretending to chat). It was pretty easy money, and there were some very good days, but the irregularity of it meant not many could really make a living from it, although some managed it. The downside was not knowing what you were doing the next day, or when you'd get home. This was of course in the days before mobile phones were commonplace, so an understanding partner and a prepaid phone card was essential.

For the first time since I was twenty-one I had cause to shave off my moustache. I'd been called to an audition where I was to be considered as a weasel in Terry Jones version of *The Wind in the Willows*. I'm not quite sure what the casting director saw in my very 'weasley' weasel, but it inspired him to cast me as a rabbit... It was going to be for several days' work over a couple of weeks, but the only caveat was that I would have to remove my moustache so that they could, and I kid you not, stick a false moustache on me. Doing so meant they could incorporate rabbit-like whiskers. I would also have a mould taken of my upper teeth in order to form the rabbit like over-dentures, and I attended a fitting for my own personal bunny ears.

I'm barely seen in the finished film, but I had a terrific time on set, and as most of the cast were former members of Monty Python (along with a sprinkling of both serious and comedy actors), I had the privilege of watching some of my favourite comedians at work up close.

While most days working 'on the crowd' were uneventful, some days were better than others. For instance, I played the chauffeur to Emilia Fox in her first film role; similarly I was a cab driver for Sam West in his first television role, and I spent a day with Jo Brand when we all travelled by minibus to the funfair location we were using. I got snogged in the street by Denise Van Outen, and then was photographed in bed between her and Julian Clary (I didn't know which way to turn!). I enjoyed a lovely chat with Julie Walters over lunch, and met Judi Dench a couple of times before she was a Dame. I also got to watch David Bowie rehearse. I was introduced to Anthony Hopkins and Max Von Sydow among others, and was directed by Richard Attenborough on several occasions, with the last occasion being the day his Knighthood was announced - a delightful man.

*   *   *

Background artists are sometimes hired by production companies to stand in for contestants or guests for the camera rehearsals for television shows. In this capacity I was often a stand-in contestant on the game show *Fifteen to One*, and twice I was an emergency audience 'plant' for the *Steve Wright People Show*.

In 1994 radio DJ Steve Wright launched an attempt at a chat show, featuring current stars, gags and audience challenges and of course, music. One of the 'zany' items was that three male audience members would be invited to carry out an unknown challenge.

For the pilot show, this gag was for the men to be dressed in lingerie especially cut for men, and return to the stage and give a 'fashion show'. My task was to be one of these volunteers for the rehearsals, and be seated in the audience during the recording and raise my hand should insufficient contestants be forthcoming.

I was dressed in a baby pink camisole bra and French knickers - but kept my white socks and Reebok trainers on. Myself and two others came on stage and gave the desired fashion show, and were interviewed by our host. This was followed by Cyndi Lauper who sang her song 'Girls Just Wanna Have Fun', and as the music began, she spotted me standing at the edge of the stage, dashed over, grabbed me by the hand and dragged me back on set, where we then both proceeded to dance and sing her best-known song – while I was wearing pink lingerie!!

(While waiting for the crew to adjust something, I found myself standing next to Paul O'Grady, who popped in from another studio at Television Centre to see what was going on. At the time Paul was best known for his drag queen alter ego Lily Savage, and rarely appeared out of costume. So here I was chatting with the most famous drag artist in the country who was wearing his civvies - while I was wearing sexy lingerie. The irony was not lost on me).

The idea went down so well that Cyndi said she would repeat this with the real audience member during the recording. And while the pilot was never aired, when the show was commissioned I went back again, but this time the band was East 17, and I don't think Brian Harvey wanted to dance with me. Again, sufficient volunteers were found for the recording, so thankfully no evidence of my involvement exists.

This source of irregular income would eventually lead to other, possibly greater things, so I'll return to this activity further on. Meanwhile…

*   *   *

While I was doing some engineering work, and the 'crowd' work, I also bought a nice grey suit and chauffeur's cap and started hiring out the Rolls as a wedding car. Another string to the bow which was not too onerous, in fact it was a pleasant way to spend a day as everyone is having such a nice time and are pleased to see you. Although it was nerve wracking every time I hit the start button on the Rolls - I was never really certain that the 1938 car would start. It never let me down though. The only downside to weddings was that I'd be booked many months, often over a year in advance, and this started to interfere with our motorsport activities. Fortunately, my old school friend Clive would step in and for a modest fee do the jobs that I couldn't cover.

Our 1938 Rolls-Royce Wraith. Many a happy bride was driven to her wedding by me

But it didn't stop there. Both my father and I had a passing interest in magic, and one visit to the magic shop in Battersea saw me leave with some modelling balloons - the sort that balloon animals were made of, and for a laugh I taught myself how to make balloon models. In my quest for larger quantities of modelling balloons I discovered a balloon decorating store, where you could be taught, and buy the supplies to create massive balloon decorations. This was something that's quite popular these days, but back then it was unusual.

I signed up for classes and became a qualified balloon decorator (only my second ever qualification!). I began yet another new venture with 'Pop Zeppelin's Balloon Works', a balloon decorating service whose name was created between myself and my signwriting friend Steve Brown - who also designed a great Pop Zeppelin character and logo for the business.

With help from Alli, we decorated weddings and other functions, and delivered 'balloons in boxes' on days such as Valentine's Day. It was a good alternative to flowers as the impact was bigger - for less money.

As if all this wasn't enough, I'd also sent an un-commissioned article on drag racing to the enthusiast magazine '*Street Machine*'. I can't recall what prompted me to do this, but I received a response from the editor, Russ Smith[10] suggesting that I might want to consider covering the major drag racing events for the magazine. So, with no real experience, I borrowed some professional camera equipment from my good friend (and former drag racer), Ron Pudney Jnr., and set sail for the 'Pod with my press credentials in hand.

As I'd been a racer I was actually quite well known to all the regular photographers, and I'm sure they saw me as an interloper with no track record (so to speak), who had nicked some of their hard to come by work. Fortunately, I managed to prove myself, and became published in other magazines too, including *Custom Car, Practical Classics,* and American periodicals *National Dragster* and *Super Stock.*

The TV programme *The Bill* was being produced from a studio not far away in Merton, and Action Vehicles were the nominated on-set vehicle supplier, with their main base being at Shepperton Studios. When in conversation with the boss Darren Litton, it became apparent that I was local to the Merton base, and he asked if I might do some driving for them there. With that, I became part of the cohort of casual drivers that they used to call upon.

The job entailed transporting vehicles - in particular police cars - to and from set, looking after them, maintaining them, and positioning them where required. And thanks to my engineering skills, I also started making safety equipment, camera mounting rigs and modifying cars and motorcycles for stunts. Much like the 'noddy' work, this was last minute and often long hours, but

---

[10] *Russ noticed that my address was in the same road as his sister, so said he'd call by next time he was visiting - and so he did, bringing sister Maddie and her fiancé Graham with him. It transpired that Maddie and Alli were 'train buddies' catching the same train in the morning from Carshalton - small world and all that. We've become very close friends since, with Graham being one of Scott's Godparents.*

unlike the 'noddy' work, we were treated as part of the crew rather than 'living furniture'.

So, here I was at this time working as an engineer, a mechanic, a TV and film extra, a wedding chauffeur, a balloon decorator, a freelance motorsport journalist and photographer, and a stand-by vehicle coordinator!

Alarm bells began to ring with the inland revenue, who called me in (with my accountant), for an interview to explain myself, as it seemed unlikely that anyone could be carrying out all these tasks, and claiming tax back on... well pretty much everything I purchased!

My accountant, John Denison, was both my father's and uncle's accountant, he'd also been the accountant that got me out of the mess that was Metmaster. Shall we just say that he worked in his clients' best interests rather than that of the Inland Revenue. When making the appointment with the tax office I was asked who the accountant was that I would be bringing with me.

'John Denison' I said.

'Oh, him,' came the reply.

I had a distinct feeling that his reputation preceded him. His son continues to look after our affairs today.

Thanks to some smooth talking and some kicks under the table from John, along with a couple of 'I think what my client is suggesting' interjections, they agreed with everything I said, and in fact I ended up with a small rebate. But to be fair, I was doing so many different things I was spending more time administering everything that actually doing the work.

Gradually some of these jobs fell by the wayside, but I think the nineties may have been the tip of my Polymath iceberg.

*   *   *

Sylvester Stallone climbed down from the set of the last scene, walked across the studio floor, shook my hand, thanked me for my work, and left the building.

Some five months earlier my presence had been requested at Shepperton Studios. I went into the production office where the meeting was to take place and decided to pop in the loo quickly to 'make myself comfortable'. While standing at the urinal Bernie Bellew came in and stood beside me - this was the very person I was here to meet. We didn't shake hands…

Bernie and I were familiar with each other from my work as a supporting artiste, and he was now the second assistant director on the upcoming blockbuster *Judge Dredd*. I can't say I'd heard of the cartoon character, but it transpired the film was to star Stallone in the lead role, and it seemed to Bernie that I might be the right sort of person to be a stand-in and double for one of the main characters - primarily by virtue of the fact I was the same height and build as the actor.

I met the producer Beau Marks and we confirmed that I'd be content to shave off my moustache (for only the second time), for the duration of the job. I was to be the stand-in[11] for American comedian and actor Rob Schneider, who was to play the comedy sidekick Herman 'Fergie' Ferguson to Stallone's role of Judge Dredd himself. My first day on set was to be a couple of weeks later.

I met Rob on the first day and we got on well, and while he'd been a star on the classic American comedy show *Saturday Night Live*, this was to be his biggest film role so far.

I'd previously met Steve Morphew on the crowd scene, and he was to be Stallone's stand-in. He'd worked regularly as a stand-in

---

[11] *A stand-in assumes the positions and recreates the actions of a main character in order for the technical crews to set up the shot and practice the camera moves. This can be a lengthy and tedious process, and using a stand-in allows the stars to relax in their trailers (and learn their lines) without having to be bothered with such tedium. Effectively being employed as a supporting artiste, the work was primarily for the camera and lighting departments. As a stand-in I was expected to be on set all day, every day that my actor was in to perform, and as Rob was a lead character, that was to be pretty much every day for the next four months.*

and quickly showed me the ropes - we got on like a house on fire.

The days were long, and as the vast majority of the filming was studio-based we were indoors most of the time and rarely seeing daylight. At least we were being fed (a little too) regularly.

I was also to be Rob's 'double' for scenes where his face wasn't seen, and when his stunt double wasn't able to be there, Marc Boyle, the stunt coordinator, asked me to carry out the 'wire work' stunts in his place. This was a sequence involving the flying bikes, where Fergie is lifted from one flying bike to another by Dredd. The wire team was excellent, but the rig I wore was uncomfortable - and with hindsight I should have worn shin pads. On one take, the timing of the bike movement (which was on a primitive computer operated gimbal), and my movement on the wire wasn't quite right, and I crashed down onto the bike severely bruising my shins. I mentioned to Bernie that this was possibly beyond my paygrade and he kindly gave me a bonus that day. It still bloody hurt though.

Some days I was used as 'utility', which basically meant doing anything I was asked. I met most of the actors and ran lines with many of them. I stood-in for the singer Ian Dury who was playing the character Geiger and enjoyed his company - he was a music legend in my eyes - and doubled for his dead body in the scene where he's been killed by the baddie Rico (played by Armand Assante). I also doubled for the dead body of a black actor who was a good six inches taller than me. During the 'block wars' in the filming, his character was shot when Dredd stormed the room, and something went wrong which injured his arm quite badly - necessitating hospital treatment. The filming needed to be completed, I put on his (baggy on me), costume, and approximated the position he assumed after being 'shot'.

It's worth reminding ourselves that this was a period of action films where all the stunts and effects were 'practical'. Digital technology at the time was primitive and expensive, so if a director wanted to blow something up, they would simply blow something up! Even green-screen effects were in their infancy. These days a realistic robot would be digitally created and dropped in, while the live actors react to a stick, or perhaps a bloke with ping pong balls stuck to him. When the ABC robot was brought to life (by the character Rico) on set, I had the privilege of being right next to it. It was a full-size giant of a robot (albeit it tethered to the ground), operated by some powerful - for the time - computers.

While I was doubling for Fergie's supposedly dead body toward the end of the film, I was showered with burning debris from the explosions around me. Daring not to move until I heard the word 'Cut' for fear of ruining the shot, some hair was singed and I received some minor burns to the back of my hands.

(Rob's mother and sister came over from the USA to visit him, I did what I could to look after them while they were on set and Rob kindly asked Alli and me to join them all for dinner at Planet Hollywood. At the time the burger chain Planet Hollywood was owned by Sylvester Stallone, Bruce Willis and Arnold Schwarzenegger, and the public would queue for hours outside to get in. Alli and I arrived by cab, dropped Rob's name to the security guy in charge of 'the rope that shall not be crossed' and were allowed in - much to the chagrin of the people at the front of the line. Rob arrived with his family a little later and we enjoyed a typical American restaurant-style meal. When I popped to the loo I was approached by a member of staff who said, 'Excuse me sir, but what does Mister Schneider actually do?' So I filled him in on the details and returned to my seat. A little while later, I felt I should pay for our meal, and rather than argue the toss with Rob, I found my friendly waiter again and proffered my credit card, only to be told, 'It's alright sir, Mister Stallone has already taken care of it'. If I'd known that I would have drunk a brandy too!!)

It was one of the many night shoots, and Steve and I were doing what we usually did, stand-in when asked and watch the monitors so we knew what was going on. Stallone would invite a girlfriend along, and she often sat and watched the action from the monitors too. Steve, being a pleasant bloke, would get the young woman coffee, chat to her, and generally keep her informed as to what was going on - as would I.

Steve got a call to go to the production office. When he returned he was furious, in his civvies, and virtually in tears.

'I've been sacked!' he said.

"Why? What for?'

'Stallone's got the hump with me chatting to his bird.'

The next day Steve had been replaced by a Spanish bodybuilder whose first language wasn't English – he had BO too…

Sylvester Stallone, insecure; who'd have thought? I made a point of not engaging with his girlfriend from then on.

*   *   *

Spending most days of nearly five months on a major film set was hugely educational, I learnt an enormous amount about how films were made, who did what - and why. I also got to closely watch actors work, and observe the process. It was around this time I had the 'I could do that' moment.

Even when I'd been doing supporting artiste work I'd noticed how the actors were chauffeured to set, and treated with a much greater degree of dignity and respect. Whereas extras were - especially on large calls - treated like cattle. The larger jobs being referred to as 'cattle calls' for a reason.

I started asking questions of cast members I'd got to know, and even the director Danny Cannon. Would I, at the age of thirty-seven, realistically be able to train as an actor? The answer was a unanimous yes. If I took some training, and built up a show-reel portfolio of work, there was no reason why not.

One actor, Huggy Leaver, told me that the best thing to do was get unpaid work on student and low budget films, which is how he came to be appearing in this very film. Huggy had worked on Danny Cannon's graduation film, and subsequently been invited to appear in Danny's first film *The Young Americans* and now *Judge Dredd*. It was to a degree, by way of repayment. Huggy also worked on Guy Ritchie's low budget short film *The Hard Case,* which led to him having a main role in the notorious *Lock Stock and Two Smoking Barrels.*

'I can do that,' I thought - as usual.

Danny Cannon directed (sic) me to the trade periodical PCR, which listed, among other things, cast and crew breakdowns for low budget and student films. The stapled together sheets were printed on red paper so that it couldn't be photocopied and freely shared. I subscribed, and among the listings came across an advert from Janey Fothergill, a casting director who was offering 'surgeries' advising actors on their career path. What I was proposing wasn't really what Janey was intending, but she saw me anyway.

I came away from her office in Goodge Street with a 'road map' of how I should go about things. She was clear that I should stop working as a supporting artist, and that there were certain things I needed to achieve to appear credible as an actor to casting directors. First, and possibly the most obvious, was to learn how to act. To this end she suggested a variety of drama schools, but generally this wasn't a viable option as I still needed to earn a wage with the variety of activities in which I remained engaged. So, it was suggested that I took private coaching, and recommended Jan Chappell as a potential teacher. I also had to get myself listed in the trade directory 'Spotlight', and to do so I needed both an agent and to be a member of Equity. It was important to do as much work as possible - the sort of low budget and student work mentioned earlier, ultimately to give me enough material to assemble a reasonable show-reel.

This was all going to be quite a challenge.

My time working as an extra, both for Action Vehicles and on *Judge Dredd,* gave me a reasonable education of the business, but one thing I knew for sure, no-one was ever going to be 'spotted' on set as an extra. I reduced the amount of supporting artist work I took substantially for the time being.

Next, the union.

Actors Equity only allows themselves to have one person of a given name in their membership - the name must be unique. There was already a Dave Gibbons, a David Gibbons, and, would you believe, a David A Gibbons, on Equity's books, so I created my alter-ego, Gibb Sutherland. Completely unintentionally I'd chanced upon a unique, and more importantly, memorable name.

I chose the name because many people called my Dad 'Gibb', and my Mum's maiden name was Sutherland. To differentiate between me and the gazillion other Daves on set, the first assistant director on Judge Dredd, Chris Newman, always called for 'Dave Gibb'.

With the name problem set aside, I now needed to have the approval on the application form of two paid up members of Equity. Fortunately, my old drag racing chum Ron Pudney Jnr. was one, having been a member in order to perform magic (his race car was called 'Magician'). The only other member I knew that I thought I might be able to call upon lived in Beechwood Court where Alli and I lived – actor Charles Pemberton. Fortunately, he obliged.

In those days, to become a member of Equity you needed to provide evidence that you had worked, and you had work booked. This was a bit of a 'Catch 22' situation, as you couldn't generally get acting work until you were a member of Equity. But, that challenge was be easier if I got work as a variety artiste. Time to fall back on a hobby!

My interest in magic, along with the subsequent addition of balloon modelling, was revived, and with some help from Ron and my dad I put together enough tricks to be able to entertain the public with close up magic. One tip that Ron gave me was 'It doesn't have to be a great trick, you don't even have to do it well, as long as it's entertaining'.

Fortunately, a couple of restaurants I frequented agreed to give me a couple of spots, and also agreed to supply contracts for three future dates. To reinforce my application, I also became a member of The Concert Artistes Association, a club in Covent Garden for acts and actors. However, in order to do so meant that I had to perform a live show on their own stage - in front of the members.

Until now my prestidigitation had been restricted to close up work - I'd never performed on stage before. Undaunted, I wrote a fifteen-minute comedy stage routine, rehearsed and practiced the gags, and went on stage.

Not having stood in front of a live audience before, let alone one entirely comprised of variety professionals - I was shitting myself. One of the tricks didn't really come off the way it should, but I managed to cover it. They laughed, they clapped - I was in.

And I was hooked.

With no track record, and no real evidence of acting at all securing an agent was proving difficult. I finally got lucky when an actor I met on a commercial while working for Action Vehicles recommended Jill Searle of The Casting Department. Jill was not by any means a mainstream agent, she didn't handle theatre, or film, and only a bit of TV. The Casting Department was primarily an agent specialising in commercials and print adverts. Better than nothing, and what's more, Jill saw something in me and took me on.

So with union card in hand, and an agent, I applied to Spotlight and became listed. Gibb Sutherland was officially an actor - who hadn't actually had an acting job!

*   *   *

During this time, I'd been travelling regularly to north London to see Jan Chappell, taking her private tuition, and joining in with group sessions she was holding. She was totally on board with what I was trying to do and fully supportive. Jan was famous for playing Cally in the cult TV series *Blake's Seven*, trained at RADA, and was a regular player at the Royal Shakespeare Company. She taught me the basics, but it was clear I was going to be 'learning on the job'. Fortunately, I'd been involved with the business for long enough to know how to 'behave like an actor'. The long and short of it was, I was getting away with it - again.

After a while Jan got the call to go back to The Royal Shakespeare Company - something to do with playing Lady Macbeth at Stratford apparently (!), but she put me in touch with

Steve Tiller, a fellow RADA graduate who was happy to continue my unconventional education in performance. The best news was that the bloke lived in Croydon.

I'm pleased to say that both of these people remain good friends today, and I love them both dearly - I owe them so much. In later years Jan went on to run her own agency. She took me on and I helped her run it, but by that time she was starting to run things down toward retirement. It became pretty much a vehicle to represent herself, her son, and me.

So, spoiler alert. I didn't become a wildly successful actor, but I won a reasonable amount of jobs. Some earned good money, some didn't.

I worked on countless student, low budget short, and feature films - well in excess of a hundred. I met some fabulously talented people, but unlike Huggy Leaver, none of them became well known and took me with them. (Coincidentally, I later bumped into Huggy and worked with him on a graduation film. He was clearly still using the same process to advance his career.)

While I'm not going to list every acting job I worked on, there are a few that stand out, and a couple of which I'm rather proud. It'll come as no surprise that I never made it to the West End stage, I did however make it to 'Off West End' in a couple of fringe shows. One was *Coffee Cigarettes and Paranoia* at The King's Head - a leading fringe venue in Islington, and another was *Warcrime*, written and directed by my now friend and acting coach Steve Tiller, a 'found space' play which we performed in the crypt of St. Andrew's Church in Holborn - very atmospheric and effectively 'in the round' layout wise. It sold well and was well received – the likes of Corin Redgrave came to watch, and I'm certain I saw Salman Rushdie in the audience.

The most successful play I worked on by far was *A Fan's Club*, which was a play about the demise of Wimbledon Football Club, it's transformation into the MK Dons, and the subsequent forming of a new club by the fans - AFC Wimbledon. This may have seemed a strange play for someone who harbours a strong dislike of the ball game known as foot, but I was to play Mr. Fran, one of the bad guys - the protagonists that broke up the club and took it to Milton Keynes. But it didn't stop the producer insisting on making me attend an AFC Wimbledon football game.

The play was performed in the Wimbledon Studio Theatre, which is attached to the main Wimbledon Theatre, the understanding being that if it performed well it would transfer to the main stage.

The cast and crew of 'A Fan's Club', that's me in the middle

The run of four weeks sold out nearly every night. The majority of the audience consisted of AFC fans, who were, shall we say, not a conventional theatre audience. It was most probably the first time many of them had set foot inside a theatre. It was amusing to see some of them returning from the bar after the interval with cases of beer, rather than a single glass.

It was a play with music (but not a musical), and there was a band on stage with us, and for the first time I had a duet to sing. A slightly daunting feature for me was that each night I performed with the well-known stage and television actor (and AFC fan) Alun Armstrong, who played 'Mr Big', a character whose entire performance was on a pre-recorded video. Not only did this require precise timing on my part, but the reliability of both the technical equipment - and the person operating it!

The show was a huge success! Yes, it was going to transfer to the main Wimbledon Theatre stage!

Everyone but the band got re-cast. That's show business I guess…

*　　　*　　　*

Television work included a couple of guest appearances on the kids' show *Chucklevision*. I was called to the BBC Television Centre to audition as a cheesemaker, once again my audition was so good that I got cast as a shopkeeper. Guest actors on *Chucklevision* were there to be the fall guy for Paul and Barry Chuckle's gags - stuff gets done to them, usually painful or mucky, or both. In this case, a cream cake in the face. Still, it was huge fun working with Paul and Barry Chuckle (not their real name, and they were actually half-brothers). The following year, out of the blue, I got a call to return for another role in the programme - no audition required - as Mr Hersey, a poor unfortunate that was at the end of everything the Chuckles did wrong. *Who's Minding the Store* and *Pretty Polly* are the two episodes in question.

There was a good number of commercials though, and several were only ever seen on the continent. Performance-wise, they may not have always been challenging, but financially usually well rewarded. Plus, there was the whole chauffeur-driven thing going on too.

One of the earliest was a commercial to launch the change of brand name from Opal Fruits to Starburst. Once again, I auditioned for one of the scientists, but got cast as a security guard (do you see a pattern here?). The role wasn't as large - in that there was no dialogue - but the pay was the same. I spent two days at Ealing Studios in order to be seen walking past a doorway, pausing, taking a bite of a banana, and walking off. I ate a lot of bananas – I don't like bananas!

In those days, actors were paid a basic studio fee, and then a repeat fee on top of that once the commercial was aired. The more it aired, the more the actor got paid. The first cheque was sufficient to buy the Formula Vauxhall Lotus race car that replaced the Formula Ford, and the second cheque bought an eight-seat dining set and a gas barbeque. Not bad for a couple of days' work…

But the writing was on the wall for repeat fees, the production companies wanted a simpler (read - cheaper) system, and Equity's negotiating teeth were no longer what they used to be. The basic studio fees remained, but the repeat fees were replaced with a one off 'buyout' which was due the moment the commercial first aired. While it was based on the *expected* showings, it was less than previously expected.

I shot several commercials that never got aired, which was a shame as the remuneration would have been substantial. When you've completed a job like that, it's hard not to spend the money in your head before you get it.

A couple of examples…

I found myself in a casting studio sitting on a chair holding an old steering wheel - pretending to drive a vintage racing car. This was to be a commercial for the Whisky giant Johnnie Walker, and little more was known than that – it was all a bit hush-hush. I had a casting recall where again I 'acted' being the driver of a vintage race car – this time for the director and the advertising agency and it was decided that, aided and abetted by my moustache, I had the look they were after. The fact that I possessed the 'special skill' of actually being able to drive a racing car was noted, but I was assured that the vehicle would be on a tracking trailer and no driving would be involved.

The commercial was to be filmed a few days later - the 22nd July - at Chalgrove Airfield in Oxfordshire, and if you were paying attention in chapter eight, you'll notice that this would also be mine and Alli's wedding anniversary, but what you won't have yet read is that this being 2005, Alli was heavily pregnant – in fact overdue.

The idea of leaving my expectant wife alone for a day wasn't appealing – to either of us, and while the basic studio fee of £350 would be useful, the buyout fee of £7000 would be more so. We decided that under the circumstances I should take the risk - and take the job.

I arrived at the location and all became clear. This was to be a commercial to announce the sponsorship tie-in of Johnnie Walker and Mercedes McLaren Formula One! The advert was to track the years of Mercedes racing from the very start, with various racing cars morphing through the years - from the original Blitzen Benz to the then current MP4-20 Formula One car. I was to be the 'driver' of the Blitzen Benz!

I was sent to wardrobe and dressed accordingly, and taken to the car to try the seat for size. A German gentleman by the name of Manfred – the engineer who maintained the vintage racing cars brought over from the Mercedes museum – showed me around the car. The other vehicles he'd brought with him included one of the famous 'Silver Arrows' which was to be driven by Aston Martin works driver Darren Turner.

Clearly, not only was Manfred allowed, but perfectly capable of driving the cars in his charge, not only that, he had the audacity to sport a moustache to rival mine! This didn't escape the notice the director, and reasoning that it would make his job much easier by having someone actually drive the car, promoted Manfred to the role of driver. The fact he possessed no acting skills, nor a member of Actors' Equity, was deemed irrelevant. I was demoted to the position of 'riding mechanic'. At least I was still in, and I'd get to be driven around in a priceless piece of automotive history! Except, in spite of being historically accurate, when the director saw the two of us crammed into the cockpit, he declared that it looked ridiculous. Manfred would drive solo.

Taken back to wardrobe I was outfitted in a new costume, and declared 'race official who paints the start-line on the track' – a far cry from what I'd been expecting. I was assured that I was to remain featured in the commercial, and that my seven grand was safe. Filming went as planned, I'd seen some iconic race cars in action, and I didn't get a call from Alli to say that she'd gone into labour. I returned home – a little dejected by the highs and lows of the day.

A few weeks later my studio fee was paid, but upon enquiring as to when the commercial would be aired (and more importantly, when I'd get my £7000!) was told that while the entire commercial had been completed (at immense cost!), it was not to be broadcast. So no buyout. At least I hadn't missed the birth of my child for it – our son was born three days later.

A couple of years earlier I'd had a similar experience. After three auditions I'd won the role of a Spanish waiter (it wouldn't be the first or last time my similarity to Fawlty Towers' Manuel would be noticed) in a Mercedes commercial. This commercial was to feature myself, and three well known 'actors' – David Coulthard, Kimi Raikkonen and Mika Hakkinen – all Mercedes representatives at the time.

They were to be seated at separate tables in a restaurant, sending more and more ridiculous items to each other. I was to be the hapless waiter trying to deal with it all – I was assured it would be hilarious. The commercial was to be filmed a week later in Barcelona - the day after the Formula One Grand Prix.

When my agent called on the Friday morning before I was due to fly out - we'd heard nothing about travel arrangements - she was told that the whole idea had been dropped. It would be an understatement to say that I was disappointed, not only would I have spent time with three legends of motor sport, and have a free trip to Barcelona, of course I wouldn't be getting the buyout fee. This being Mercedes the commercial was due to be aired world-wide, and subsequently the buyout had been set a handsome £35,000… At least I got twenty-five quid for the second audition recall.

And people wonder why I don't like Mercedes.

*   *   *

Unlike some previous auditions, I attended one to be cast as a naturist, and for a change that's exactly the role I was given. But to be fair, there was more than one of us. Again, a non-speaking role, but it involved me feeding a horse with a carrot - while I was naked. It was the closing shot of a commercial for internet service provider Freeserve, and the only thing to cover my dignity would be a digitally applied logo. A friend of mine saw this commercial in a cinema - I appeared about twelve feet tall.

Once you've been seen naked on TV there's not a lot you won't do…

*   *   *

Twixt the time I was giving up 'crowd work' and moving into 'serious acting' work, whilst sitting on the set as a supporting artist on *Red Dwarf*, the idea came upon me that if the kids I'd been making short films for could do it, why couldn't I? It would be a good way to showcase my acting and provide material for a show reel - perhaps even get the film screened at festivals.

I was with some of the regular crowd that I knew, including Howard Whiteson and Paul Keys. Howard was an aspiring writer, and Paul had been a child actor. We bounced around a few ideas, and based entirely on what I could lay my hands on as far as location, sets, vehicles etc., Howard wrote a script to order.

The Job was a twenty-minute film about four police officers who amuse themselves at weekends by planning a bank job. Using the contacts I had made while working on *Judge Dredd*, I managed to rustle up a professional crew, who brought with them some professional equipment. Just like actors, crew also use material they have worked on to help move them up the industry ladder. Bob Bridges had been the video coordinator on Dredd, his own connections provided much of the lighting and camera equipment for free - and I couldn't have made the film without him.

Over three days we would shoot the film. Bob would film the exteriors and direct the interior scenes, while Mario Mooney would handle the sound department. We also had the benefit of Sharon Mansfield, a professional script supervisor, and a contact through my old friend Ian Caple put me in touch with musicians Mick Corr and Tony Warburton, who wrote original rights-free music especially for the film.

140

My connections with Action Vehicles supplied the police uniforms and police car we needed, while our flat provided the interior location and permission was obtained to use the exterior of both my local bank and police station.

My acting teacher Steve Tiller would play one of the characters, while myself, Howard, Paul, and a friend of an actor I'd met previously, Rosemary Johnson, would fill the other main roles. A couple of friends from the crowd helped out in the background too.

With a cast and crew in excess of twelve people, Alli stepped in to take the most important job of all – catering! I figured if these people were working for nothing, the least I could do was feed them well - and Alli came up with the goods.

Once all the footage was shot, Bob then handled the editing in an editing suite that he part-owned at Pinewood Studios. These days you would be able to handle all the editing on using the phone that's in your pocket, but in 1998, it took a huge amount of processing power provided by two large computers.

We screened the finished film at The Charles Cryer Theatre in Carshalton and it was well received, and some of us used the footage to try and move our careers forward, but the upshot was that the film remained for the most part, unseen. Bob went on to be the video coordinator on all of the *Harry Potter* films - his work on *The Job*[12] would have nothing to do with it.

I'm very proud of what we produced though, and will always be grateful to all of those that helped. It was huge fun, hard work, and an education.

* * *

Some work that gave me an enormous amount of pleasure was playing Manuel in a *Fawlty Towers* dinner show. Three of us, Basil, Cybil, and myself, would attend a restaurant or hotel and interact with the guests over a three-course meal. It was part improvisation and part scripted, and we always adapted the

---

[12] *The finished film 'The Job' is available to view on Vimeo.*

material to suit the venue and the guests. We'd help serve and clear the tables, while performing versions of the famous routines from the famous television series. Manuel was always popular, but of course went through a good deal of abuse and slapstick punishment at the hands of Basil Fawlty. It was two hours' very hard work, much of it physical, but enormous fun. The pay was atrocious, but the pleasure given to the guests made it all worthwhile. For me, making people laugh was what performing was all about.

'Is not easy for me Mr Fawlty!'

I did this for a couple of years from late 2012, and to be fair I was a little on the old side to be playing Manuel - I was dying my hair and moustache for the job, but, if I say so myself, I was pretty good at it. The pay was poor for the amount of time involved, driving to and from the gig always took a while and would involve the M25, and I'm diligent enough to always get there early, but occasionally there would be an overnight or two.

One 'Basil' I worked with liked a drink after the show, as indeed did I - often it would be with the guests. But on this occasion Basil and I were sharing a room. He came to bed in the early hours of the morning blind drunk. I won't recount the details here, but it's safe to say it was a disturbed night. Unable to rouse him in the morning, he missed breakfast, and we were late on leaving for the journey home. The following day I told the producer what had happened, and that I wasn't prepared to share a room with anyone in future. He told me that he wasn't prepared to have anyone tell him how to run his business.

The services of Manuel were no longer required and I hung up the white jacket.

Without proper representation, and now living in deepest Kent, it became difficult to obtain acting work, so I've pretty much given up on that as a career now, but it's something I enjoy, and it's something I can do. I've come to realise that to succeed as a performer you not only need a certain amount of luck, you need to have a passion for it - you need to *live* for performing. And I don't have that.

But never say never, I figure all the time I can walk and talk, I can act. In the meantime, I keep my Spotlight and Equity subscriptions up to date.

* * *

So, there I was, standing dressed head to foot in a black Lycra bodysuit, when George Lucas entered the room.

I imagine you may have just adopted a quizzical look at this last paragraph.

I was at Leavesden studios, where the majority of the crew that had worked on *Judge Dredd* were now involved with *Star Wars - Part One* (later to be re-named *The Phantom Menace*). Bernie Bellew needed someone he knew he could rely on, give a performance, and do what was required without making a fuss. So he called me in to be 'Ree Yees', a Gran alien.

While visual effects were making massive advances, like Judge Dredd much of what was being filmed had to be 'practical' in nature, and filmed in front of a green screen. There were to be some digitally enhanced characters, but Ree Yees and two other Gran were deemed to be of the 'blokes in suits' variety.

Most of the other creatures were humanoid in shape and heads and arms put onto a person while they wore a costume. The Gran creature was the only creature created that consisted of an all-encompassing body suit - the black Lycra suit was what everything would be attached to.

The details were incredible, with small foam pieces added to the limbs and fingers to give a sense of muscle texture. A mould of my head and face was taken so that a glassfibre helmet could be made which would be firmly attached so that when I moved my head, the Gran head would move correctly, rather than have my head just wobble around inside a mask. I would effectively be moving the head with the bridge of my nose. One of the heads for the character Mawhonic would have animatronics fitted, but that would be worn by a member of the creature department who were constructing the suits. There were three Gran in total, myself, the animatronics version, and Martin Virgo, a supporting artist also known to Bernie.

I had seven or eight fittings for the body, and a couple more for the costumes it wore. While I was doing this, I was also working for Action Vehicles at the Brent Cross Shopping Centre in North London.

*   *   *

Having earlier helped prepare some of the stunt cars, I was working as one of the vehicle coordinators on the James Bond film *Tomorrow Never Dies*. The job entailed looking after the fifteen BMW 750i hero cars that were there for the shoot, as well as the various other cars that the baddies would drive - and crash.

Three of the cars were 'invisible driver' cars where a stuntman sat on the floor of the rear of the car and drove it using remote controls, while watching three monitor screens that were fed from three small cameras hidden inside the door and driving mirrors - the monitors were monochrome too, as this pre-dated small LCD colour screens.

Three other cars were fitted with the gadgets that Bond would operate, while the remaining ten were simply 'doubles'. Each time a car got damaged during the chase - for instance a bazooka rocket gets fired through the front and rear screens - it was my task to replicate the damage on all fourteen of the other cars. When Pierce Brosnan had to drive the car, I would place it and return it to its first position - Pierce wasn't keen on reversing...

There was one incident where a baddies' car would be towed by a cable into a parked car - and there would be an explosion. The car caught fire as expected, and on cue the fire crew moved in to extinguish the flames - only there was nothing coming forth from their hoses. The fire was getting bigger. I bravely left the building.[13]

I remain amused each time I see the film when the bad guys try to get into Bond's BMW in the car park, and in failing they finally empty their machine guns onto it, and by the magic of cinema, the car rocks back and forth as the bullets hit. That was me crouched down at the back of the car and shaking it by the rear bumper!

So for three weeks I found myself bouncing back and forth between the vehicle base at Radlett Airfield, Brent Cross Shopping Centre, and Leavesden Studios - it was a busy time.

*   *   *

A little bit of air between takes

A Gran is a bulky creature, not unlike a Sumo Wrestler, it also has three eyes and a nose not unlike that of a camel, and as I mentioned earlier, the body was fully enclosed with only a small aperture in the mouth to enable breathing. And when the clothes were added it got even hotter in there - very hot indeed. Quite correctly, the production team had identified that this may be a problem, and stipulated that no-one was to be in the suit for more than forty-five minutes, isotonic drinks would be available throughout, cool air would be blown into the mouth of

---

[13] *I was the first one out and watched the inferno develop from ground level, and the remaining crew joined me - while the entire Brent Cross Shopping Centre was evacuated. Eventually control was taken, and the 'real' fire brigade attended, but the event damaged a good deal of that floor of the multi-storey car park. The production team simply moved the set to another floor while they paid for the damage to be repaired.*

the creature when not shooting, and that there would be medics with oxygen standing by. Confidence inspiring it was not.

There was only one shooting day where all three Gran were seen together, a couple of days of myself and Martin, and the rest, just me. I think I shot for ten days altogether, the last of which was for the second unit - and I was suffering with food poisoning. The idea of being in that suit and not being able to get out *very* quickly wasn't appealing. (Fortunately, second unit first assistant director Nick Heckstall-Smith was very understanding, and disaster averted).

On one of the early days of the shoot, Terence Stamp was unhappy about having to deliver his dialogue to a cross on a stick on the far side of the sound stage, and he couldn't hear the script supervisor read the 'missing' actors' lines without any 'performance'. With the knowledge that I could both give a performance and my voice would carry, Bernie Bellew replaced the cross on a stick with me, on a scaffold tower. I did the same thing for several of the main cast, including Ian McDiarmid, and while my work will never be seen, it was a privilege to work with a couple of our greatest actors.

I bumped into Terence as he was leaving the studio, and he was kind enough to say, 'Thank you for that dear boy, I couldn't have done it without you.'

I never was a *Star Wars* fan, and so remain. When I told everyone I was involved in Episode One, I couldn't really understand what all the fuss was about - surely this was just another overblown production - little more than a cowboy film set in space! What I didn't expect was to be approached by fans for autographs.

A few years after the film was released, I received an email from the Belgian Star Wars fan club, asking what my requirements would be to attend a signing in Brussels. At first, I thought it was some kind of joke, but after speaking with Alli about it I responded with what I considered a rather cheeky reply.

'Two return tickets on the Eurostar, and two nights all expenses paid in a hotel in the heart of Brussels.'

'No problem,' came back the reply, 'When can you be here?'

With that Alli and I enjoyed a splendid weekend in Brussels in a glorious hotel being treated like royalty by the two leading members of the fan club. In return, all I was asked to do was sign a few posters, cards and photos, and be photographed doing so. This led to a request to attend a collectors' convention at Sandown Park for two days to sign autographs.

I'd never seen anything like it, there were rows and rows of stands selling all manner of film memorabilia, and table upon table of minor celebrities signing autographs - and I was one of them. I was seated next to Bond girl Madeline Smith, who had appeared in *Live and Let Die*. It was her first convention too, and she was a delightful lady with whom to spend a couple of days. To be fair, she was more popular than me and did more 'trade', but I'd made the right decision by asking for a flat fee rather than a 'per autograph' arrangement. The organiser had arranged for there to be a couple of hundred copies of a still taken from *The Phantom Menace* featuring Ree Yees available for me to sign - I still have most of them….

It was clear that there was a 'hierarchy' at these affairs, where the size of your role in a production dictated your stature, and as my role as Ree Yees was uncredited, and my face wasn't recognisable, I was a bloody long way down the list.

That would be my one and only convention. The best part for me though, was 'meeting' Mickey Rooney.

Hollywood legend Mickey Rooney was another attending the convention and signing autographs. He was taking a break in a hallway with his eighth wife Jan Chamberlain (I can only imagine that he was having to do this to pay alimony to the previous seven wives!), and I had to pass them on the way to the bathroom. They were alone at the time, I smiled at him and he called to me, 'Hey, no-one seems to want to speak with us.' I told him I'd love to stop but I was busting for a pee, and I'd stop on the way back. Sadly, when I returned, they were gone.

As for Star Wars – I still don't get it…

*   *   *

Clearly happy with what I'd done on the Bond film, Action Vehicle boss Darren Litton trusted me to be the vehicle co-ordinator on the first series of the lesser-known TV comedy *The Last Salute*.

Shot in 1997, it was set in the late fifties and early sixties when the AA men got about on motorbike and sidecar and would salute members on the road if they were displaying an AA badge on their vehicle. How quaint.

Not only was I responsible for all the vehicles on set, I had to assemble eight 'background' AA bikes from a pile of BSA A10 motorcycles Darren managed to acquire, along with a similar quantity of discarded sidecar frames. We also had access to three AA 'outfits' from museums, and one rival RAC version.

During a couple weeks at the Action Vehicles Shepperton base before the shoot, I assembled the eight bikes and sidecars and got them all running - the equipment boxes for the sidecar frames would be provided and fitted by the art department. Once completed I transported them all to the location base.

Supporting artists had been hired to ride the bikes in shot, those that had the 'special skill' on their resume of 'possessing a motorcycle licence'. Having plenty of experience with extras, I wasn't fooled and knew what to expect. While every one of them possessed a motorcycle licence, not one of them had ridden an outfit, or ridden a bike with a kick start, nor had any experience of an early motorbike with a right-hand-side gear change and left-hand-side foot brake - unlike a modern bike!

I was assured that most of the time the bikes would be 'set dressing' and only one or two would be needed to be running at any one time. Fortunately, most days I had the assistance of Toby, another Action Vehicles regular, however on the day I could have done with him being there…

The director had the fabulous idea of having all the bikes arrive outside the front of the 'AA headquarters' (actually a disused water works). I placed all eight bikes on set, instructed the riders on the vagaries of riding an outfit, how to use a kick start -

basically how to start an old banger of a motorbike that would barely run in the first place. They were after all, a bunch of scrap bikes I'd just about managed to get going - for the lowest possible cost.

Keeping them all running for long enough to get the shot was a challenge akin to spinning plates. As fast as I got one going, another one stalled, but get the scene we did.

Apart from the food poisoning I got on set (not for the first time), it was a reasonably fulfilling job. Glad of the experience, I was not in any particular rush to have that responsibility again.

12

Best laid plans and all that

We read all the books (actually Alli read most of them), and we went to the classes, both the NHS ante-natal and the National Childbirth Trust (NCT) classes. The latter were run by Katy, and as the NCT is a charity we 'made a donation' or, in my language, 'paid' for the classes. They were held at Katy's home, and, by and large excellent. Our group of five very pleasant couples learnt a great deal about what to expect as first-time parents, not just the messy bits, the pain, the nappy changing, the pain, and what to expect, but financial implications and the question of child care was raised – and did I mention the pain? The NHS classes were not only less conveniently held during the day, the group was larger, and I felt that we were all being spoken to as if we were all a little - bit - simple. However, this in fact, was a valid reaction to some of those in attendance - I also objected to having to pay 20p for the tea. Tea at Katy's was inclusive, and always came to me in a 'clip-clop horsey' mug.

Alli is ten days overdue, it's in the diary, '2 o'clock in the afternoon, baby expected, home in time for tea' - splendid. Of course, it was never going to happen like that. We tried to kick it all off by taking a long walk, which is just one of the suggested methods, others included, eating curry, eating fresh (must be fresh - not tinned) pineapple and having sex. Apparently, having sex works because semen releases oxytocin into the bloodstream which can bring on contractions. Katy told us that research has shown that semen is more easily absorbed through the lining of the stomach... We - sorry, correction - my wife - decided that the researcher must have been a man and I was duly dispatched to procure a pineapple. No-one knows exactly what pineapple contains that can trigger contractions, but I reason that it's the same thing that makes it impossible to set in jelly. That alone has always made me suspicious of pineapple and it didn't seem to work anyway.

It's Sunday morning, and my wife wakes at the ungodly hour of 4 a.m. We're already sleep deprived as on the Friday evening, our neighbour's son who returned from a year in Australia, re-acquainted himself with his friends outside on the patio, it being the height of summer. Of course, he was still on Oz time, causing my wife to go into the garden at two in the morning and tell him to shut the fuck up. Which, to his credit he did. On Saturday night however, his parents decided they too would like to welcome the wayfaring son home by throwing a party in his honour – again, outside, on the patio. We chose to roast in our bedroom with the window closed, which barely helped. So, as I say, we wake at 4 a.m. and Alli tells me that she's bleeding a little. So, I check in the 'Haynes Baby Owner's Manual', and unsurprisingly discover that this is 'not a good thing'. We 'phone St. Helier hospital and they concur, we must go in – *now*.

As all the books will advise you, along with anyone who's ever heard of someone having a baby, we've packed a bag, well, most of one, because much of what we will need is in constant use. Between us we gather up the items on the substantially comprehensive list and leave for the maternity ward – besides, we're quite sure that nothing's wrong and someone will say 'No, that's fine' and send us home in time for breakfast. I'm a trifle concerned as I'm not convinced that the alcohol I consumed the evening before had completed its journey through my system. I convince myself that I'm OK and we set sail.

Less than three quarters of an hour after waking up we're at the door of the maternity unit, where I was born 48 years before. We are warmly welcomed and taken, somewhat alarmingly, straight to a delivery suite. The midwife checks Alli over and takes a good look at our 'birth plan'. This, is a somewhat larger self-created document than the scrap of paper we had been given by the hospital to complete which really didn't adequately cover our expectations. It was to the midwife's credit that she didn't instantly roll about on the floor in hysterics, but I'm sure it allowed for some hilarity in the privacy of the nurses' station. Why do I say this you may ask? Well, it was now 5.30 a.m. and it was quite clear that there was no way we were going home without a baby, that the bleeding was a cause for concern, Alli was having contractions which, to everyone's surprise, she couldn't feel, and that this was now a medical, rather than the natural birth for which we had hoped. So, while the birth plan metaphorically turned to confetti, it remained a useful tool in as much as each midwife studied it carefully, and while things weren't going according to the plan, it gave them an insight to our desires, wishes and personality. Subsequently we were treated accordingly. To anyone who has yet to go through this process I recommend that you write a carefully worded birth plan…!

As this was now a medical birth it also became clear that Alli was going to stay in at least overnight after the arrival. Fortunately, I had the presence of mind (under the circumstances no mean feat), to check if the only private room in the maternity ward was available, and book it. This is another thing on the top of my top tips list – have a private room if you can. The privacy it afforded us after the event was invaluable – it was the best £80 I've ever spent.

A monitoring belt was strapped around Alli's waist and we could see the baby's heartbeat and the length and strength of the contractions. I was now sent back home for the handful of things we'd failed to pack. When I returned little had changed other than a shift-change for the midwife and nursing staff, but progress was being made. My wife was now feeling the contractions and tried various methods of pain relief, starting with sitting on a birthing ball, then using a TENS machine, then gas and air, occasionally opting for all three at the same time, and all had a benefit to some degree.

There had been no more bleeding, but the dreaded word 'Caesarean' had been mentioned. We were approaching midday and it was suggested that the pregnancy should be induced, something with which we had no problem, however we hadn't realised that induction came with greater pain and that they wouldn't like to administer it without an epidural. We discussed this at some length, the thought of an injection in the spine and its associated, although rare, risks were not appealing. We were told that it would be better to have the injection now while my wife was experiencing little pain and still able to move freely, rather than later while she may not be able to stay still. This all made sense and we went ahead, before we knew it the epidural was in and so was the Syntocinon drip.

Unfortunately, two of the main side effects of the epidural are nausea, chills and shivers, both of which my wife suffered. Her lips turned blue and she was wrapped in layer upon layer of blankets, and yes, she was sick. Eventually this passed and while she stayed as mobile as possible – mainly on the birth ball - she finally became confined to the bed and the contractions were coming thick and fast. Then we lost the baby's heartbeat.

Registrars were summoned, one of whom appeared to have a scalpel behind his back muttering something about C-section. Another realised that a new machine known as STAN was available, it was the only one in the hospital and not only could it more easily monitor the baby's heartbeat and my wife's contractions, but also worked as an ECG machine ensuring the baby was not in distress. This was duly attached (a clip is affixed to the poor little mite's head!), and all was well. The registrar sighed, put his knife away and left. There was a moment when we considered calling the baby Stan – but only a moment!

It's midnight, and we've been through an entire set of shift changes, we now have midwife number four, Sue. She tells us that we've progressed far enough and will want Alli to start pushing in an hour, and stops the epidural so the contractions could be felt. An hour later, the waters have been broken and we're off, the pushing has begun. My initial reaction is that this can't possibly work, my wife has subsequently told me that the same thought went through her mind. If, after an hour of pushing the baby's still not here, forceps or ventouse will be considered. The pushing continues with no small amount of support and encouragement from Sue, who, throughout was an absolute star. She understood our wishes for the baby to arrive naturally, and she was going to do her level best to make sure that it happened that way.

An hour passed, still no baby, and the registrar was put on standby. Sue bought us another fifteen minutes, then another. The man with the knife was now standing in the room with a pair of forceps not very well hidden behind his back. Sue buys us more time but Alli was getting weak and the epidural wearing off. Sue does half a top up on the epidural in preparation for the forceps, and opens up the registrar's bag of tools. My wife feels another contraction and Sue tells her to use it – the head is nearly out. Sue turns to the registrar and says, no, make that, *tells him*, 'Shall I?' The registrar nods and makes discreet, but not discreet enough, scissors action with his fingers. Sue rips open her own bag of tools, administers a cut and with a push...

I feel like I'm in a dream, none of this is real and I'm watching it all from above, maybe it's the sleep deprivation, maybe the adrenaline – or both. Alli is, to put it bluntly, fucked, we're both in tears and all I can say is 'Oh my God, it's our baby, it's our baby'. That thing about being invited to cut the cord was never going to happen.

The baby was out but not breathing. The umbilical cord was around its neck as were its hands - as if the baby was trying to get the cord off itself. Things began to move with more than a degree of urgency, the baby was put in a basket, the airways cleared and oxygen given as the nurses did what was necessary to get the child to breathe. After what seemed an eternity but was only a minute (literally a lifetime for the baby), there was a cry. The registrar put down the forceps and gave me a thumbs up.

Meanwhile, Alli is in poor shape. The snip to help the birth became a tear, and she was losing a lot of blood. Frankly, I couldn't watch. The registrar stepped in to deliver the placenta when I heard him say 'Oh, I've haven't seen that before, have you?' showing it to the nurse. She answered in the negative and it was decided that it was an abnormality that needed further investigation, but not before Alli gave permission to do so - because the placenta technically belonged to her.

Permission granted, it was set aside to await shipment to the appropriate experts - we were never to discover what was so unusual.

Meanwhile, the delivery room was looking like a scene from *Reservoir Dogs*. Having delivered the mutant placenta, the registrar moved in again to repair the damage to Alli, while nurses feverishly assisted - or mopped up the blood.

I suddenly realised we didn't even know what sex the baby was.

'What have we got?'

The midwife replied, 'Didn't you see? It's a boy, a beautiful boy.'

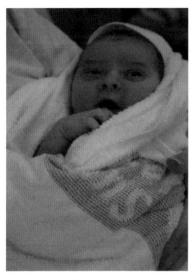

It took a while before it was deemed that all was fine with our son, but eventually the midwife took the boy from the basket, gave him to Alli.

'Does he have a name?' she asked.

We glanced at each other just to confirm.

'Yes, he's called Scott.'

I have no words to describe the joy I felt at that moment.

Scott – day one

Welcome to the world Scott Daniel Gibbons. 8lb 7oz, born 25th July 2005. 2.45am!

There remained concerns about body temperature for some time, so he was kept in an incubator or snuggled up with Alli. The midwife asked if we'd like something to eat and she brought us tea and toast. It was only cheap sliced white, but it was the best toast we've ever eaten.

We'd both been awake since four o'clock the previous morning. I was shattered - Alli of course, even more so. Alli was moved into the private room already mentioned, with access to a private bathroom and we were kept busy with regular check-ups on both mother and baby. I called all those that needed to know.

Evening arrived and it became clear that we weren't going home together tonight - I reluctantly went home to sleep alone.

The following morning, well rested, I returned to St. Helier Hospital and eventually we were given the all clear to go home. I popped down to the car to get the baby carrier and returned to the ward, pressing the security intercom buzzer to gain access I was asked.

'Who is it please?'

'It's Dave Gibbons, and I've come to collect my wife and son.' I broke into tears.

It suddenly dawned on me that we had a son.

13

Careless or unlucky?

When I was a child I had relative success in receiving head injuries, the first being when I rode my rocking horse down the front steps of our house. Then as mentioned in Chapter Three, when I slipped off of the rear seat of our first Rolls-Royce when Dad braked heavily - the mechanical brake servo on pre-war Rolls is particularly efficient... Soon after, when leaving Wallington Town Hall after an unsuccessful meeting with a district nurse, my mum stormed out of the main doors. As she opened the door the leading edge met my head just above my eye (if you've witnessed a boxing match, that particular area of the head can produce a copious quantity of blood). I got patched up by the very person Mum had just rowed with!

The most notable head injury occurred while I was at summer scout camp. Tents had been erected in a clearing in some woods, and I busied myself chopping wood for the fire as instructed. I'm not sure that these days anyone would leave a twelve-year-old unsupervised while in charge of a sharp axe, but there you go.

Two of the 'Sixers' (those scouts being charged with the command of a group of six), were having some fun while I was minding my own business with the axe. One sixer let the other's tent down - unhappiness ensued. The culprit ran past me, while the affronted Boy Scout threw a large mallet after him. I popped my head up to see what all the fuss was about, and smack… the mallet hit me square in the middle of my forehead.

When I came to, the scout leader was doing his best to remain calm, and staunch the flow of blood from the gaping wound. Apparently, it hit me with such force my feet left the ground. Fortunately, the axe didn't cause any further damage!

My parents joined me at the hospital following eight stitches to my forehead. I'm sure they must have used some anaesthetic, but it didn't actually feel like it - I'd never felt pain like that before.

So that was the end of my summer camp - and I hadn't even spent a night away from home. I returned to school with a sticking plaster on my head, and persistent headaches dogged me for months.

I'm fairly certain the only reason I was sent to the 3rd. Wallington Scout Group was so that my parents could have some 'private time', likewise Sunday School, as I don't recall ever asking to go to either, and I certainly didn't enjoy either. Even at that young age I was questioning the plausibility of some of the stories in the Bible - I wasn't good Christian material, and at Scouts, all the other kids wanted to do was play football at every opportunity. I hated football then - still do.

What is surprising is that at the time, it was perfectly acceptable for eleven to sixteen-year-old kids to wander the streets each armed with a Bowie knife attached to their belt - a knife with a five-inch blade. Yes, we'd play with them, and throw them, and sharpen them, but at no time do I recall it being a threat to society, or anyone getting hurt by one of them. In spite of us throwing them into the floor beside each other's feet to see how close we could get.

In a similar vein, my father had a small collection of antique guns. Not that he ever used them, the engineer in him enjoyed the way they functioned. One of these weapons was a Naval Colt 45 revolver - just like the guns they used in Westerns.

When I was thirteen I took it to school for a show and tell. In my duffle bag. On the bus. And no-one batted an eyelid…

I escaped injury for a while after that, until the winter of 1983. Snow was on the ground, and I was sitting in the hire shop with my dad, and thanks to the weather business was slow and we were both pretty fed up.

'Sod it,' said Dad 'get that battery off the truck and we'll get it charged.'

I braved the snow outside and removed the flat battery from the truck and carried it into the shop. The snow that had compacted on my boots met the lino floor of the shop and my feet went from under me. Into the air went the battery, I landed flat on my back, and the battery returned to earth landing on my right hand. I carefully removed my glove and my ring finger remained barely attached to my hand.

Climbing over the driver's seat into the passenger seat because the passenger door didn't open, we got into the Pontiac Sunbird we had at the time (a truly horrid four- cylinder American compact car), and made our way slowly - due to the icy roads - to St. Helier hospital.

These days few would not sing the praises of the NHS – but this was not my experience at the time. They sewed up the damaged flesh as best they could, and that on the adjacent finger too, bound my two middle fingers together for support, and sent me home. With instructions to exercise the finger by squeezing a foam ball to ensure the joint would continue to function, and to return in a week's time.

Four days later there was an almighty 'crack' sound from my finger as I squeezed the ball, accompanied by some degree of pain. I returned to the hospital where I was seen by the consultant who upon inspecting the damage was more than somewhat alarmed, saying that I should have been shown to him immediately and that there was no choice but to have me into hospital and operate.

Two days' later I was in, and the procedure completed. My finger was cut open and a stainless-steel pin used to thread all the bits of the broken bone back together, once it was sewn back up my hand was bound so that all the fingers were kept separate but supported.

When I came to from the anaesthetic, I questioned the position of the fingertips poking out of the bandages - they looked odd, but I was assured that everything was as it should be. I was to return in three weeks for removal of the bandage and stitches.

'Oh,' said the nurse as she revealed my hand. As I'd suspected, my repaired ring finger was pointing at a somewhat jaunty angle. I was taken to the consultant.

'Ah,' he said 'I wasn't expecting that.'

At no point did anyone accept any responsibility, but it became clear after an x-ray, that whoever bandaged my hand had rotated my finger on the pin, and in the process displaced some of the broken pieces - undoing all the good work the consultant had done. And now it was firmly fixed in place.

They tried to kid me that by strapping my two fingers together tightly that it would pull back around, and that hot wax therapy and ice water therapy were going to encourage the joint back into motion. It was a waste of time, and I knew it.

I considered some sort of recourse, but the advice was that it was impossible to successfully sue the NHS, and besides, the only thing that could be done would be to cosmetically straighten the finger - the joint would never work again.

I gave up, and I've put up with a dodgy finger ever since. Dad always felt guilty about it, as it was his insistence that we got something done that day. Years later he offered to pay for the finger to be straightened, but the fact remained, the finger could be made to look better but it would never function. I decided that it wasn't worth the time, nuisance and discomfort.

*   *   *

Alli was three months pregnant, it was January, and I was painting the side of our house in Springfield Road. I'd already painted the front, but took the opportunity to share scaffolding with our next-door neighbour who was having an extension built.

It was cold, wet and icy outside, and not really the weather conducive to the work, but I needed to get the job done while the scaffold was available to us. Coming back down I stepped across to the ladder - and lost my footing. I fell ten feet landing on my back on the dwarf wall between the properties and rolled on the ground. Mark was a local handyman and had been helping me, he heard the shout, found me, and alerted Alli. My back hurt a lot, I'd been winded and had trouble breathing. An ambulance was called.

Fifty minutes later the ambulance arrived, the medics found me wrapped in a blanket on the ground. Common sense told me not to move, but I don't think I could have anyway. A 'scoop' stretcher was used to lift me from my landing spot into the ambulance and I was taken - very gently - to St. Helier Hospital.

Once in the treatment room all of my clothing was cut from me, and my neck chain and wedding ring removed. They took all of my possessions and gave them to Alli, she later told me it felt like an 'I'm sorry, there was nothing we could do' moment!

Several nurses were in attendance and they carefully rolled me onto my side - and someone put their finger up my bum. Apparently, they were checking the coccyx. Under the circumstances some kind of warning would have been nice…

I was moved onto a gurney and rolled off to x-ray. The doctor in charge was a little miffed at the state of his treatment room. Where the paramedics had scooped me up in our front garden, they also scooped up a large quantity of dead wisteria leaves, which were now scattered with abandon all across the once pristine room.

I'd fractured L4 and L5 vertebrae, and there was nothing for it but to give me pain killers and order a complete body brace to be fitted. I was not to try and move unaided until the brace had arrived and been fitted by the orthopaedic department.

The days went by and no body brace was forthcoming. Fortunately, I'd been given a room on my own as they didn't want to risk anything or anyone else banging into me, and a portable TV was found for me. The worst part was needing assistance to go to the toilet while lying down, and subsequently be cleaned up. The agency night nurses really weren't happy to do this at all.

Three days later there was still no sign of the body brace, and I received many stories of 'Oh well, it has to be made,' and so on. But I persisted in asking. It transpired that the hospital was part of a 'trust' of several hospitals, and my brace had in fact been supplied – but to Epsom General Hospital, about ten miles away. It seemed to me that the obvious thing to do was to go and get it. But no, another one was ordered.

It arrived three days later, but no-one from the orthopaedic department was available until the next day to fit it. I was to be allowed to remove it at night as long as I slept on my back and never moved - if I needed to stand up, the brace needed to be on. Alli was on hand to be trained in the fitting and removal process. The brace was made up of several pieces of hard plastic, removable pads of foam, and a lot of Velcro straps. The orthopaedic nurses clearly had no idea what to do with this thing and had never seen one before. Alli read the instructions and told them what to do. Once I could demonstrate that I could walk and climb stairs I was allowed home - the evening before my birthday.

Once again, I felt I'd been let down by what is generally perceived to be an excellent National Health Service. The daft part is, we were covered by private medical insurance, but they wouldn't transfer me to another hospital for fear of further injury.

*   *   *

Dad kept himself active and busy in his later years - aged 78 he was still riding his Harley Davidson. Mum had been teaching him to fend for himself as her emphysema was getting worse, she could only get about on a mobility scooter and she was in fear of dying and leaving Dad on his own. Injuries sustained from being knocked from that very scooter had set her back substantially.

Dad had been suffering a few complaints, he'd received a shoulder injury from falling from a sailboard which finally got the treatment it required (you may see the irony in this later). A blood test at one point discovered lymphoma, which can be life shortening, but it was deemed not to be of concern, and that the likelihood was that Dad would die of something else first! He was also being treated for a renal disorder, with twice weekly visits to St. Helier Hospital.

One night he woke with a 'rattling' in his chest, which caused both Mum and Dad concern. They were both already unwell with flu-like symptoms so they called us – we decided to visit. Clearly Dad was very unwell, so we called for an ambulance. As he was already under the renal unit, he was admitted there and tests were carried out and antibiotics given.

It was pneumonia, and his condition was quickly worsening.

The signals from the doctor weren't good, and suggested that my Mum really ought to be there. Alli went and got her, quickly returning with Mum in a wheelchair her still dressed in her night-wear.

Finally, a decision was made to take Dad into intensive care, induce a coma so that fierce antibiotics could be administered, allowing his immune system to function as best it could. He was wheeled away.

'I'll kick this,' he said as the gurney left the room. Little did I know at the time, they were the last words I'd hear from my dad.

Alli and I took Mum back to her home and settled her in, and then we went home ourselves. During the night she had a panic attack, and couldn't breathe, and sensibly called an ambulance. We went back to St. Helier. I now had both my parents in the same hospital at the same time - just in different wards.

I bounced back and forth between the wards to check on both of them, and stayed the following night, sleeping on a bench in the family room provided by the ICU. Both wards were keeping me updated on my mobile phone, which at the time were not allowed to be used in hospitals (there was a fear that the signals interfered with medical equipment), but it was the only way I could be contacted and was insistent that it was vital for me to have it with me.

It was St. George's Day, and in the morning, I went to see Mum. She was more comfortable and breathing well enough, and as I sat there next to her my phone rang. A nurse shot me a look of displeasure.

'Hello Mr Gibbons, this is the ICU, he's gone.' I told Mum.

I went to see Dad before I left, made sure Mum was okay, and went home.

*   *   *

Mum ploughed on, and we fitted equipment in the house to aid with mobility - a stair lift had been installed long before Dad passed away. With an increasing dependence on oxygen, her home was plumbed with an oxygen generator with an outlet in every room. When she left the house, oxygen came from a cylinder which was carried on the back of her mobility scooter.

She tried to keep active, and had a good network of friends locally who helped where they could and kept her spirits up. Mum always loved the garden and flowers, and did what she could in the garden to occupy herself, until she had a fall and managed to drag herself back indoors to raise the alarm. After that, she was given a personal alarm button.

Each visit to the hospital set her back even further, and every day was a struggle. I visited one day, and noticed bandages on both of her wrists. She tried to hide them from me - perhaps deliberately not too well. Alli and I went to her doctor's surgery, and did battle with the receptionist, insisting that clearly, she'd attempted to take her own life. Eventually the message got through and the doctor made a visit. Apparently, she'd also taken a large quantity of paracetamol too.

It's not until you witness such things you realise how truly horrid life must have been for her. I hoped that the fact that Scott was with us by this time may have given her a reason to carry on, but clearly that wasn't enough.

A short while later respite care at a local hospice was discussed. It was proffered as a temporary measure, something to help redress the balance and give her a break from the daily struggle. So, to St. Raphael's Hospice she went, and enjoyed a lovely room overlooking a delightful garden. We'd visit with Scott, who at only six months old was a big hit with the nurses. The care was exemplary, but her breathing was getting worse - a nurse warned me that Mum may not leave the St. Raphael's as initially expected.

In the early hours of the morning of the fifteenth of February I was woken by the ringing phone - it was the hospice. Four years on from my father, my mother had now gone too. I suspect that the hospice, while not assisting, didn't prevent her passing, helping her on her way and making it as peaceful as it could be.

*   *   *

We'd been sitting in the waiting area for three hours, the (extortionate and unnecessary) car park charges were racking up, and I'd read all of the out of date magazines. Surely if it was bad news they wouldn't make us wait this long.

Yes, they would.

Alli had reported a lump in her breast to our doctor, she'd had a biopsy, and now we were at the Kent & Canterbury Hospital waiting for the results. We'd already seen one couple leave in tears, now it was our turn. The nurse finally called us in to see the registrar, and with pleasantries completed he read the notes - you might have thought he'd have done that before we got in there, but no.

'I'm sorry, but yes, it's cancer,' he said, matter of factly.

At this point I'm not going to even try to tell you how Alli must have felt - that's her story, but I just went cold, did my best to support, and help ask all the right questions. In these situations, we've always found that two heads are better than one.

What I learnt very quickly is that everyone's cancer is different, it affects them differently, and their treatment is different. We were given an outline of what might happen next. Removal of the breast was a given, as was the chemotherapy that would follow.

We were directed to the resident Macmillan nurse.

She was very good, and gave all the support and information she could, then Alli mentioned that we had private health cover. At that point the nurse directed us to the Chaucer Hospital, and that was our last interaction we the Macmillan nurse. I'm sure they do fantastic work, but I guess they would prefer to save their services for those that can't afford it.

The next hours, days, weeks and months were a blur. Alli researched the hell out of everything, managed to remain positive, and maintained the position that she was going to get through this and come out of the other side. Well, that was the impression she gave. I tried to do the same, but I had some very dark moments. Scott was only three years old, and I suspect that the thought of leaving him without a mother was all the driving force my wife needed.

The Chaucer was contacted and a consultant found. Fortunately, Chaucer is a Centre of Excellence for cancer treatment, and the consultant a leader in the field. I've come to discover however, that wherever I've had treatment for whatever medical issue, this always seems to be the case. In this instance though it appeared to be true, the treatment and care given were second to none.

Each step of the process was seen as the next goal, first the surgery to remove the breast, then the chemo, and later there would be radiology too. The chemo was horrid. I'd sit with Alli at the hospital while it was administered, and bring home what looked like a ghost. All the while we had to keep away from infection as her immune system was depleted to virtually nil - very difficult when you have a three-year-old at nursery bringing home who knows what bugs. One thing that became clear though early on, was that Alli wouldn't now have to go through the pesky nuisance of the menopause and the chemotherapy would make her infertile.

As predicted, Alli's hair began to fall out. We were directed to a specialist wig supplier, and once a suitable wig was chosen and made, the lady shaved the remaining hair off of Alli's head and fitted the wig. It was a good effort, but it really wasn't the same - Scott wasn't sure about it at all. Alli only really wore the wig in public when necessary, but occasionally went out wearing a bandana. At the time we had a customised pick-up truck - alloy wheels, lowered, trick paint, and tinted windows. I remember watching Alli drive off in the truck one day with a bandana in place - she looked really cool.

After countless treatments, examinations, check-ups and procedures, things had gone well enough that it was deemed a suitable time to consider breast replacement surgery. Again, we went to a Centre of Excellence (the McIndoe Centre at the Queen Victoria Hospital in East Grinstead), and a leader in the field of breast reconstruction. I have to say that I was somewhat taken aback with what the lady consultant proposed - it all seemed a bit 'Doctor Frankenstein' to me.

They were to take the skin and fatty tissue from Alli's tummy, and use this to form and create a replacement breast, they would also have to recreate a belly button. This was also to be a very lengthy surgical procedure, but the added bonus was - a tummy tuck!

Alli was adamant that this was the way forward, and we planned for the procedure to take place over the Christmas of 2009. The hospital was in East Grinstead, so Scott and I would stay with friends in Brighton (and by the way, at the Theatre Royal, we enjoyed the best *Peter Pan* pantomime I've ever seen). The surgery was successful and the recovery lengthy.

There was the option of using a stick-on nipple, or at a later date having a nipple formed from the skin. Hence, I found myself helping choose the location of the new nipple, bearing in mind that nipples vary from side to side anyway. With location chosen and marked, the same surgeon carried out the procedure, and later it was pigmented with a tattoo for improved 'authenticity'. Yes, there is a good deal of scarring, and a whole bunch of flesh without sensation, but the reality is that the whole procedure was a success, and looks (almost) natural.

Of course, it's no spoiler to mention that all of my wife's treatment for cancer was successful. She had to take a tablet every day for ten years, but now everything in that department is gladly back to normal. I have a happy healthy wife and I couldn't be more proud of Alli for going through what she did, and her determination to not let cancer win.

*   *   *

I was seated next to Maurice in the Bedford Hospital. My nails were covered in chequered pattern nail transfers - it had been raining at Santa Pod the day before and I thought it might be something fun to do! A family seated across from us were there with a couple of kids, also waiting. One of the kids wanted something to eat, the dad got up, walked to the vending machine, grabbed it by the top and shook it vigorously until something fell into the tray beneath. He took the chocolate bar and gave it to the kid. The nurse on reception said and did nothing and I wasn't about to either. I was there because I'd just had the most unexciting motor sport accident ever - I'd been run over by my own race car.

You may have read earlier in Chapter Five, that my heel got caught under the rear wheel of my dragster, which came to a halt on top of both of my feet. After the screaming in agony stopped, the track's medics were called in their ambulance, and after a quick assessment took me to Santa Pod's medical centre to see the doctor. He made me stand and try to go on tiptoe - which was excruciating in both feet, and concluded that there was no serious damage and gave me some strong painkillers - I even had the presence of mind to check that they weren't on the banned medication list in case I was going to be able to carry on racing.

Mark the Medic got me back to the ambulance and took me back to our pit area and helped me into the caravan.

'Go to the hospital,' he said. 'Get it checked out.'

Maurice and Alli retrieved the race car from where we'd left it, and then Maurice drove me to the hospital leaving Alli and Scott at the track.

So we found ourselves in the waiting room, which is exactly what we did - wait. Others that came in after me got seen before me, and I can only assume that on the face of it, their ailments appeared worse than mine. Finally, I got taken to a treatment room, and then to x-ray.

'I know you can't give me a medical opinion on what you've just seen,' I said to the radiologist, 'but can you give me a clue?'

'Don't bother putting your shoes and socks back on,' came the reply.

Of course, this happened on a Sunday, so there were no consultants available, so it was going to be a patch up job at best. The doctor told me that I'd pretty much powdered the navicular in my right foot - apparently a significant injury, along with a crack in the heel and damage to several metatarsals. The left foot fared slightly better - I'd only damaged a few minor bones.

And the Pod's doctor had said I should be alright to drive again tomorrow. Hmmm – I wasn't convinced...

Racer's nails!

When it comes to these sorts of things, my default position is to use humour, and I had a good laugh with all of the nurses, some of whom were particularly taken with my chequered nails.

I was offered the choice of staying there until Tuesday (it was a Bank Holiday weekend), when I could be seen by a consultant, but it was considered best that I was dealt with closer to home. They patched me up, gave me some painkillers and some crutches, and sent me on my way with instructions to go to my own local hospital as soon as I could.

At this point having an insurance broker (John Price, who was for many years also the commentator at Santa Pod), as a close friend became highly beneficial, as I managed to get Maurice insured to drive the race truck home, while Alli drove Maurice's people-carrier towing our caravan.

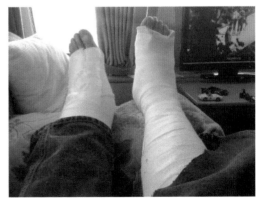

With previous experiences in mind, we decided to swerve

I wasn't going to get very far on these

169

the NHS and pull the BUPA trigger as soon as we could, and got to see a leader in the field of feet at the Chaucer Hospital on Tuesday morning. Mr. Louette wanted to operate as soon as possible before bones started setting themselves back together - in the wrong order.

With copious screws and pins he rebuilt what was left of my navicular, manipulated metatarsals, and set my right foot in plaster. The left foot was manipulated and heavily strapped. The logic being that I wasn't about to stand on either foot, so the left could look after itself.

With a subsequent procedure to remove screws, I found myself in a wheelchair for twelve weeks. Followed by a surgical boot for a further six. The summer of 2013 was a bit shit.

A couple of years later I was still having a good deal of discomfort in my right foot, and it turned out that a piece of my heel was still floating about - the tendon to which it was attached hadn't allowed it to set. Mr. Louette went back in and fixed that too - a further six weeks of nuisance.

Both feet still give me discomfort today - I suspect this will always be so.

*   *   *

The adverts say 'You should have gone to Specsavers'; well I'm glad I took note. I was having my annual check-up at the Ashford branch, when the optician told me that she thought she could see signs of 'AV nipping' and referred me to an ophthalmologist for further checks.

As the checks involved some eye drops that meant I may not be able to drive after, I was advised to have someone with me. I was welcomed by Rashid Zia (another leader in the field), who noticed my Rough Diamond Racing jacket and shirt, and it transpired that he was a car guy owning several modified and stupid-fast German cars. He was going about his business and we were chatting about fuel injection, turbocharging and engine management, when his tone suddenly changed.

'Ah,' he said. 'I can't see any evidence of AV nipping, but we need to have a conversation.'

Sensing that this may be a situation where two heads are better than one.

'Shall I call my wife in?' I replied.

Alli came in and Rashid continued.

'It's a good job you've been referred to me. You have something known as acute angle glaucoma. It's a condition where the fluid passages in the eye aren't working correctly and a sudden increase in pressure with the eye can occur. This could happen at any time. You would suffer a headache that won't respond to treatment, nausea, and within an hour you would go blind in both eyes. The trouble is…'

And here was the kicker,

'… the drops I just put in your eyes can trigger it.'

Well that was a surprise and no mistake.

'So what do we do now?'

'Go and have a cup of coffee. If you feel a headache coming on, or you feel unwell, get back here as fast as you can as we'll have a medical emergency on our hands.'

So Alli and I went to Sainsbury's coffee shop, and waited. All the time I was thinking, 'Is that a headache coming on, am I feeling a bit queasy?'

After the longest hour *ever* with no sign of any symptoms, we returned. The temporary cure was to laser channels through the iris to create channels for the fluid to pass around the eye. Rashid wasn't equipped to do this so referred me to a specialist. It would be four to six weeks before the treatment could be carried out by the NHS, but I wasn't sure that I could live with the thought that I might go blind at any moment for that long. So once again we pulled the BUPA trigger and it was done in four days.

It was a strange sensation, with each zap of the laser resulting in an unpleasant cracking noise and the feeling of someone flicking the inside of my skull at the back and centre of my head. There is a slim chance that I may still be afflicted, so I'm now considering lens replacement, as that will remove the risk completely.

*   *   *

There have been a few other medical procedures. In 2015 while on holiday in Jersey I got pitched off of a 'Flowrider' - basically a static surfing machine. Having mastered all the tricks while kneeling and lying down, I progressed to proper standing up surfing, only for the board to leave at great speed from beneath my feet, pitching me up in the air, culminating in a hard landing on my shoulder.

A visit to our local minor injuries' unit gave the diagnosis that it was a 'rotator cuff injury' and would get better in time. It didn't, two years later the discomfort continued, and seeking out Mr. Relwani – yes, another 'leader in the field' - it became apparent that I had a tear to the tendon in my shoulder. The surgery to repair the damage was significant and would take a good deal of time to recover. The advice was, if I could live with the pain - do so.

My sixtieth birthday fell during this time, and I'd suggested to Alli that I'd rather like to have a go at Speedway riding. Reluctantly she relented, and a 'Ride and Slide' speedway experience was booked. I had a fantastic time, but the task of moving my weight back and forth on the bike really took its toll on my shoulders, and I pretty much collapsed onto the handlebars as I stopped the bike on my last lap.

Scott was watching, but it's probably fortunate that he didn't immediately want to try it himself, but anyone with a passing interest in motor sport really should have a go at Speedway.

I have no desire to fling myself out of a perfectly serviceable airplane, but the idea of indoor skydiving appealed. Again citing 'the dodgy shoulder' as a reason for me not to do it, Alli eventually agreed, with all three of us taking in the experience at

Milton Keynes. If I'd known what lay in the future I may not have been so gung-ho with either of these activities.

Eighteen months after Mr. Relwani's diagnosis I fell from a step-ladder while pruning a grapevine - I landed in exactly the same way as I did on the Flowrider.

The long and short of it was that the tear I already had was now a complete rip - and the MRI scan proved it. Imagine if you can, a tear in a sheet of paper, once it's started, it's much easier to completely rip the paper apart. And so it was.

Mr. Relwani described it as a 'significant injury', and unless I was happy to live in considerable pain for the rest of my days, surgery was the only option. The resulting surgery resulted in twelve weeks of not being able to drive, and having my arm in a sling. And as I write this, I'm still undergoing physiotherapy to regain the strength in my arm.

Alli no longer allows me to do anything that may even remotely result in injury; even standing on a stool to change a lightbulb is now frowned upon.

Apparently, having a go on the wall of death or a luge skeleton is out of the question…

14

Calling a variety of cars

The Isle of Man is not noted for its car manufacturing, but in 1964 the Peel Motor Company manufactured their second car. The Peel Trident was the successor to the Peel P50, and was an improvement in that two (admittedly small and friendly), people could fit inside. It was like an Isetta bubble car, but smaller - if you can believe it, three-wheeled and powered by a 49cc DKW two-stroke motor. It had a clear bubble dome to protect the residents from the elements, a three-speed transmission, and resembled the sort of flying car that might have been used by 'The Jetsons'. With a top speed of about 35mph, the manufacturer advertised it as 'almost cheaper than walking'!

It must have been about 1970 when Dad acquired one from I don't know where. We took the dome off and picked it up and carried it on its side through our side gate. Once in the garden, my school friend Mike Charman and I made my best attempts at achieving its theoretical top speed on the lawn, occasionally tipping it on its side. It wasn't a very big garden.

There were number plates on it, but it was never used on the road, in fact I don't believe Dad had any paperwork for it, and suspect that it may have been 'misappropriated' by one of the shadier customers of the hire shop. So, it's very likely that my first 'hot car' may have been hot in more ways than one. One day it was gone as miraculously as it had appeared.

The first car I actually remember travelling in was the one that Mum used on my first day at school. It was a pale yellow-and-white Austin Metropolitan, with white-wall tyres and a removable hardtop. These cars were manufactured by Nash in the USA, assembled in the UK by Austin of England, and used Austin's 1500cc 'B' series engine. The design was something that these days one might describe as 'Marmite' in style - either you like it, or you don't - and looked as though it should be able to float. I distinctly remember the plastic black-and-white 'hounds-tooth' chequered upholstery. Apparently when Dad bought it, he

174

insisted the dealer throw his leather sheepskin coat into the bargain. Another car I'd like to have now.

The Metropolitan was shortly followed by a 1960 Chevrolet Impala, fitted with a 'Blue-Flame' six cylinder engine and a power-glide gearbox. This car also had white-wall tyres and, like every other car we owned around that time, was used to tow Dad's hydroplane. Somewhat troubling is that in those days dedicated tow bars were rare, and one simply bolted a tow ball onto the car's bumper and off you went (although car bumpers were much studier affairs back then!). I also believe that the right-hand-drive conversion on this particular example of Chevrolet involved a system of chains behind the dashboard...

The 1960 Chevrolet Impala outside 63 Ross Road. I've no idea who that is in the hydroplane!

As mentioned in Chapter Seven, my first 'proper' car was a 1964 Hillman Super Minx, it was automatic - and a convertible! Dad bought it for me for my seventeenth birthday, and once I fixed the transmission problem that it came with (and made it cheap), it was a fun car to drive. I've always been a fan of top down motoring and it started right here.

I 'customised' it as best I could with what I could afford. It received some self-adhesive pinstripes, and a 'jack-up kit' on the rear springs to make space for the massive pair of rear wheels and tyres that I'd acquired. Eventually a completely unnecessary and non-functioning 'pro-stock' drag race style bonnet scoop also graced its bonnet. It must have looked ridiculous.

One of the few photos I have that include my first car - a Hillman Super Minx, here being used as a push car for 'Wild Angel'. I'm not sure if that's me or Dad in the driving seat

I sold that to my friend Clive, and bought a 1956 Volkswagen Beetle. It came to me 'pre-customised', with wide Weller wheels, flared fibreglass wheel arches, dark Perspex windows, racing bucket seats, and hand painted in blue Hammerite. I finished the look off by trimming the interior with deep-buttoned green velour door panels, and yellow shag pile synthetic fur glued (using Evo-Stick – I was high on the fumes for days) to all remaining interior surfaces. The rear seats had been removed to create what can only be described as something akin to a tart's boudoir. Thankfully, there are no photographs.

This was the car I drove while dating the God-fearing Fiona, and it was in the day when it was appropriate - and often expected, for a gentleman to open the car door for a lady. I tried not to laugh as Fiona attempted - and failed, to enter and exit the bucket seat while wearing a short skirt with any modicum of dignity. God only knows what she thought of that car.

The Beetle moved on when I bought the two-tone pink 1963 PA Vauxhall Cresta mentioned in Chapter Seven.

I left this car pretty much alone, with the only 'customisation' being the addition of twin aerials on the rear wings, and what were sometimes called 'shit lights' or more correctly 'cruising lights.' These were lights fitted underneath the car that shone on the ground so it looked like the car was travelling on a carpet of light. It was a popular thing to do at the time, but...

My Pink PA Cresta and my friend Len Fiddimore's supercharged Frog-Eye Sprite

The Cresta featured a two-tone grey leather interior, a 'three on the tree' three-speed column mounted gear change, and a front bench seat, and in these days before mandatory seat belts, a girlfriend could snuggle up close. Petrol was cheap, and we would drive for miles just for the sake of it. These really were the great days of motoring as far as I was concerned, never to be re-captured.

In these fledgling days of hot rods and custom cars, the Chelsea Cruise nights had only just begun. Cars of all types would gather on Chelsea and Battersea bridges once a month, and in the early days Battersea Park itself was open for use too. As the name suggests, cars would cruise the streets of the area, often taking in the King's Road, or park up where drivers would make conversation with those of like mind.

It was on one of these nights that I parked up behind two other PA Crestas, one red, and one black, both 'jacked up in back' with big wheels fitted. I engaged the owners in conversation, one was a long-haired ginger fella - Dick Hogben, and the other had more of a teddy-boy look - he was Dick's cousin, Paul 'Spunky' Mortimer. We chatted about cars and drag racing, and I happened to mention that I worked in Wallington with my Dad - and thought no more of it.

One day a short while later while at the shop, a blue Transit 'Luton' van pulled up, and out stepped Dick. At the time he was working as a delivery driver for a stationery company and happened to be in the area. Little did I know that from that day on we'd be the firmest of friends, having adventures and road trips together, and often laughing so much that our stomachs would hurt.

Dick started to come drag racing with us and took the role of crew-chief, and while he's not been able to be there for every run I've made, he's been at the majority of them - and there's no-one I'd rather have standing beside me on the start-line - particularly when performing a flame burnout!

Dick was also a roadie for a rock band (I think owning a van may have helped there), and introduced me to 'pub rock', a genre of music of which I soon became enthusiastic and remain so to this day. Up until then I'd been brought up on the likes of T Rex, Slade, and other music I'd seen on *Top of the Pops* during the early seventies - the music which was popular while I was at school. The only live bands I'd seen up to that point were Kenny Ball's Jazzmen and George Melly and John Chilton's Feetwarmers. This was at the time when punk was just kicking off, and the music scene was as exciting as it had ever been. The Ramones, Suzi and the Banshees, The Boomtown Rats, and Eddie and the Hot Rods were all on the list of groups we'd go and watch together, with a particular visit to see Motorhead being an event that I still believe to be the start of my hearing loss and tinnitus – although it's highly possible that the drag racing may have had something to do with it as well!

The PA Cresta made way for an even older E Series Vauxhall Velox. This one I didn't leave alone, and during the heatwave summer of 1976 I swapped the asthmatic straight six with a more modern and more powerful 3 litre V6 from a Ford Granada, complete with its automatic transmission, and a stronger rear axle from a PB Cresta. I'd previously sprayed the car cherry red, and Mike Charman added some custom touches to the paintwork. It was pretty quick and I used up a few tyres performing burnouts. I decided to sell it after I jacked it up one day, and rather than raise itself gracefully into the air, the jack found its way through the corroded sub-frame…

Around this same time, I'd bought a Model 'T bucket' Ford hot rod unfinished project that someone had found too much for them. Most of it was there, but it needed assembling, painting, plumbing and wiring. The engine supplied was a 1500cc pre-crossflow four-cylinder Ford engine, so not very powerful, but in something this small and light it was always going to be lively. In dark blue that I sprayed myself, Mike Charman was once again called in to create a mural on each side of the car. It turned out to be the most fun you could have in a car. I went everywhere in it, turning heads wherever I went - it was not a car for the shy. I now also had a version of the car I'd promised myself all those years before at the kart track.

The Ford Model 'T' Hot Rod I built

Peter Pitts, who went on to sponsor my Topolino dragster and help establish Metmaster, had designs on owning the 'T' so that he could keep it at his home on Alderney. He asked how much I wanted for it, and I gave him a ridiculous price. Unfortunately, it was a price he paid without batting an eyelid. I put the 'T bucket' on a trailer and towed it to the docks. A few years later it came back to the mainland and I had an opportunity to buy it back, sadly I simply couldn't afford it at the time.

*   *   *

One day we found ourselves pulling an old Jaguar out of the front garden of a council house in Carshalton. Dad spotted it while delivering something from the hire shop in the same street and 'door-stepped' the owner to see if it was for sale.

It turned out to be a 1948 Jaguar XK120 Roadster; the engine had seized, which was why it was sat in the front garden of this house for so many years. With it parked on the forecourt of our hire shop, we pulled the cylinder head and sump off, removed the pistons, had the cylinder bores honed in situ, and rebuilt the engine. Once we had it running Dad asked one of our friendly local bodywork 'experts' to repaint the dull metallic bronze paintwork with an Old English White. It wasn't a great job, but overall the car was presentable and ran well - and at eighteen years of age I was driving this fabulous sucker around! (This was the car that you will have read elsewhere involved in the unrequited meeting with Debbie).

Once again, this was a case of selling a car without really trying. There was an enquiry, a high figure was given, and the vendor paid in full straight away and drove it off. It wasn't until many years later that I realised what we'd had. It was an early aluminium bodied car, one of only 240 made. Today these cars fetch money deep into the six-figure range.

Steve Thompson was an American car specialist operating out of a garage in Thornton Heath, with close links to American Autoparts who were our tenants at the time. Steve had a buyer for our Pontiac Le Mans, but rather than part with money, he wanted to part exchange it with another car. Dad had to part with a little bit of cash too, but he was quite taken with the car Steve was offering. It was a 1970 Dodge Challenger 440 R/T Magnum, featuring a four-speed manual gearbox with a Hurst pistol grip slap-stick shifter. And it was convertible too. The only thing that would make it more desirable today would be the 426 'Hemi' motor option.

It was a monster of a car to drive, great in a straight line but good for little else apart from scaring ourselves rigid. This was another that was sold against our will.

A couple of fellas came into the hire shop and asked if the Dodge was for sale. Dad said he wasn't for selling, but they persisted and he gave them a ride round the block - with the hood down.

'How much do you want Reg?'

'Two and half grand,' he replied.

'Give him the money,' one said to the other.

That too is now a car that would be approaching six figures if it were sold today.

In a similar vein, I never really forgave Dad for *not* buying a slightly damaged 1963 split window Corvette Sting Ray we were once offered by Vic Cooper. It was fitted with a factory fuel injected 327 cubic inch motor and four-speed manual transmission - this was 1976 and £350 was deemed too much. Of course, I still have the 1978 Corvette that I eventually bought with the proceeds from selling the dragster to Tony in 1984, and I can't see myself selling it anytime soon. It's a lovely car, but it ain't no '63 Split Window...

Vic Cooper, also known to us as 'Lovely Victor' due to his long blonde locks, was a businessman who occasionally hired from us, but also shared an interest in 'unusual' vehicles. One day he pulled up and parked a sleek low-slung sports car in the kerb outside the shop - I put the kettle on. Giving him his mug of tea. I said,

'What's that, some kind of VW kit car?' (They were popular at the time).

181

'Fuck off, that's a Lamborghini Espada!'

One time he turned up in a 289 AC Cobra and offered me a ride. I accepted. Closing the passenger door felt like shutting a postage stamp behind you, there was virtually no weight to it at all. What followed was a white-knuckle trip around the streets of Wallington. I believe the ulterior motive was to have me convince my dad to buy it - he didn't.

A couple of times Vic might sell a car on quickly to raise the money to help pay his staff wages, but for some reason one day he had nothing Dad wanted, so he simply lent Vic £600. And Vic went on 'the missing list' for a good while after.

The hire shop runabout at the time was a short wheelbase Land Rover which we kept in the station car park at the top of the approach. One morning it wasn't there.

The following day Vic appeared driving a long wheelbase 'Safari' Land Rover, pushed an envelope containing £600 into Dad's hand and tossed him the keys to the Land Rover, with instructions to use it until we were sorted out. We ended up buying the Landie from him, but Dad had written off the money he'd lent.

Anyway, faith in human nature restored.

*   *   *

I was on a solo visit to the USA in the spring of 1980 (I occasionally went alone - opportunities more readily arise for a lone traveller), and went to visit the shipping partner who supplied the UK speed shop Speed and Spares America. The proprietor, Chris Hext, bought a 1979 Z28 Chevrolet Camaro, and needed to get it back to the UK. The suggestion was that I extend my vacation and drive the six-month-old car from Los Angeles to New York where I would leave it to be shipped. This would be cheaper and quicker than shipping from a west coast port.

With international travel at the time - thanks to Laker Airways - being more like buying a train ticket, the travel arrangements were easy. I collected the car and set sail, with little more than a big paper map of the United States. With almost 2,500 miles to travel, I took the shortest route I could find, and intended to do it in the fewest days, staying in motels as and when I found them. One night this plan fell foul, as the sleepy town I found myself at nine o'clock in the evening had no rooms available, and as the police took a dim view of 'vagrants' sleeping in their car I continued driving through the night and stopping earlier in the day to ensure a hotel room.

Bear in mind that this was during the time when the USA's knee jerk reaction to the oil crisis was to impose a nation-wide speed limit of fifty-five miles per hour. This was not going to be as swift as it might be. But at least the car had cruise control.

During the journey, the speedo suddenly plummeted to zero, and the cruise switched itself off. The speedo cable between the gearbox and the cruise control unit had broken. No cruise control now.

I found a garage, who directed me to another garage, who might just have what I wanted in stock. I crawled under the car, replaced the drive and went on my way - and with relief, giving it a 'bit of a leg full' as I re-joined the I-40 freeway. I noticed flashing lights in the rear-view mirror, and thought I better pull over.

The officer came to the driver's window and asked me if I knew I'd been speeding - there was no point denying it. I said that I'd not seen him, and was told that he'd been alerted by an 'eye in the sky' helicopter. Realising I was English, and looking at my UK and International driving licences, he decided that the paperwork would be too much for him.

'Keep it on the double nickels' he said, and sent me on my way.

I stopped at Albuquerque, went through Amarillo, Oklahoma City, and Memphis, stopped briefly in Nashville (I thought I ought to), and continued through Knoxville, stopping for a final decent break in Roanoke, Virginia. Once refreshed I got up early and drove the last leg to New York.

Snow was now falling, not heavily, but enough to be disconcerting when you're trying to find your way around New York using only a map of the entire continent. I got properly lost a couple of times, but eventually found the area I was looking for. Parking wasn't easy, but I came across a piece of ground that clearly had recently been the site of a building. The sign said 'Car Park' - I pulled in.

Manned by two giant men who appeared to have no necks, I gave them the money and locked the car. I was told in no uncertain terms that I should leave it unlocked with the keys in the ignition. I wasn't terribly comfortable with that idea, leaving a nearly new Z28, which wasn't mine, in the middle of New York open with the keys in it sounded like a one-way ticket to disaster - but argue with these fellas I did not.

I found the office of Aaaaacon Shipping (they wanted to be sure they were first in the Yellow Pages!), dealt with the paperwork, retrieved the car from the car park (it was still there!) and took it to the shipping agent's own underground car park - again leaving it with the keys in the ignition. I grabbed my bag and thought I'd have a look around the city.

I was cold, it was snowing, I was carrying my luggage, the streets were dirty. I saw nothing of the city, and within thirty minutes of aimless wandering I hailed a Yellow Cab which took me to JFK Airport, booked a Laker ticket and got out of town as quickly as possible.

A couple of weeks later Chris collected his Z28 from the docks.

*   *   *

Another vehicle we shouldn't have let go was the 1937 Alvis Speed 25 Charlesworth Saloon. I can't recall where we got it from, but it needed some restoration, and Dad really didn't want to put the work into it, so we took the rear bumper off to use on the Rolls and let it go. It would be worth a small fortune now.

Having now mentioned the Rolls, I should explain further. I was sixteen-years-old when we spotted a damaged Rolls-Royce on the forecourt of a garage on the border of Wallington and

One (of many) that got away - Alvis Speed 25

Hackbridge, and Dad, who had always regretted selling his first Rolls-Royce (the one he owned when we lived on the St. Helier Estate), made further inquiries.

The 1938 Rolls-Royce Wraith had been involved in an accident. It transpired that the driver was drunk and hit two cars, ending up in a brick wall. The front driver's side corner was a mess, with the front wing rolled up into a ball by the driver's door, and the wheel and chassis set at what can only be described as a 'jaunty' angle.

£106 later (including the outstanding accident recovery fee), the Rolls was in our driveway. We dismantled the front end, removed all the independent suspension (the Wraith was the first Rolls-Royce model to be so equipped), and straightened the chassis using a good deal of heat, cutting and welding. We managed to source a used suspension unit from a Rolls-Royce specialist breakers yard, which was a huge amount of work to remove at the yard using the minimal tools that we had brought with us.

The damaged grille shell was sent away for repair, and a traditional coachbuilder formed a new wing from aluminium by taking measurements from the opposite side. He didn't even have the car at his works, and after trial fitting it only needed a couple of minor adjustments to fit perfectly. I'm not sure skills such as this remain in existence today. I remember Dad unusually splashed out a good deal of money on a high-quality paint job - and he got what he wanted.

Finally, it was on the road. It turned out to be only the second Wraith produced, and only recently I discovered that it had been the personal transport of Rolls-Royce CEO Lord Ernest Hives, and had been re-bodied after World War II.

We used it as our transport frequently and took it to a few local shows. We also drove it up the test hill and around the remaining banking at Brooklands. It appeared in the film *The Last Viceroy* as Mountbatten's personal car (with me appearing for the first time on TV as his chauffeur), and it was the wedding car I used later on.

This is one car that didn't get accidentally sold. It remains (albeit looking rather forlorn), in my workshop awaiting recommissioning after a lengthy lay-up, but this is one car that I am adamant will not be sold in my lifetime.

During the time we were rebuilding the Rolls, Dad spotted an old car being towed up to Curley Day's scrap yard to the rear of our shop - he went to investigate. It turned out to be a 1934 Triumph Southern Cross, an open top four-seater roadster, and it had been dragged out from under a collapsed garage from where it had been for about twenty-five years. Dad paid a little more than scrap value for it, plus the delivery to drop it in our driveway. He gave it to me for my sixteenth birthday!

It was in need of full restoration, but we got it running after I discovered that two of the plug leads had been incorrectly installed into the distributor (driven off the back of the dynamo it turned in the opposite rotation to most cars), which was probably why the car had been abandoned all those years ago. We drove it up and down Ross Road a couple of times just to make sure the drivetrain all worked as expected, and parked it under a tarpaulin. I made a start on the restoration, stripping off some of the many coats of paint, and cutting some new timber floor panels, but other things, like drag racing and girls got in the way and the work stalled.

We moved the Triumph from place to place over the years, storing it in various garages or under various tarpaulins - its condition getting no better all the time. After the demise of Metmaster, and once my workshop was built, I made a start on it again, removing the engine and gearbox, but again the work stalled. Dad eventually had it towed to his garage in West Street. He'd recently occupied himself by restoring a couple of motorcycles and thought he'd make a fresh start on it for me. He completely dismantled the car with all good intentions, removing the body and axles from the chassis, and making a photographic

record as he went. Soon after, he died.

I had the parts brought down to Kent when we moved here with all intentions of continuing the project, but with so much going on it never happened - all I was doing was shifting it round from shed to garage and back again.

Triumph Southern Cross, about 27 years after my Dad bought it for me

My main issue was that it was going to cost me more to restore than it would actually be worth when complete (in spite of it being one of only twelve remaining world-wide), and I eventually came to the realisation that despite the emotional attachment, I was never going to do it. What I *was* about to do though, was build Scott a junior dragster. I sold the Triumph to my good friend Mark Cocklin, and used the proceeds to pay for the materials to build Scott's race car. Mark sold it on too, and I've recently been contacted by the new owner who is in the process of restoration - and he's sent photographs to prove it. It's good to know that it looks like it will eventually be back on the road.

It was 1987, and I was having a fresh MOT put on the Metmaster van. A few doors down the street from the MOT station was a motorcycle shop specialising in custom bikes. So, I popped along to have a look. It turned out it was run by a chap by the name of Percy, and in fact we had some mutual friends in common.

There was a bike there that caught my eye, and for the life of me I can't remember what possessed me to do so, especially bearing in mind I had no motorcycle licence - I enquired as to the price. The owner was asking £600. And again, for a reason that's beyond me, I told Percy I only had three hundred and fifty quid to spend. He took my phone number saying that if anything turned up that I might be able to afford he would get in touch. I left the shop, got in my freshly MOT'd van, and went back to work thinking no more of it.

Some four weeks later the phone rang - it was Percy.

'That bloke's desperate for money, he'll take your £350.'

'Ah, okaaaaay,' I said, surprising myself even further by continuing, 'I'll come and get it.'

I rolled the bike out of the van and into the kerb outside the workshop. I was now the proud owner of a 1975 Triumph Bonneville T140 chopper, hardtail, six inch over forks, pull-back 'bars, and custom flame paint on a peanut tank.

With no licence to ride it...

Dad was a motorcyclist at heart, but hadn't owned a motorbike since just before I was born. It transpired that he didn't want to encourage me onto a motorbike because they were 'too dangerous', which also explains why he was so keen to get me off of a moped. He thought I was potty, but then again, it was exactly the sort of potty thing he would do.

I took and passed my motorcycle test soon after, and the very first motorbike I rode was the chopper - not exactly a beginners' bike.

Dad realised that now I was thirty years of age, I could probably make up my own mind as to whether or not I should ride a motorcycle. So, he shipped a motorcycle back from the USA on his next visit, and start riding again - later he would ship two more

My 750cc Triumph Bonneville chopper - the ideal first motorbike?

bikes back, a Honda Shadow and the Harley Davidson which I still own.

I was in the Metmaster office at the back of the workshop when Mark Cocklin (the chap who later bought the Southern Cross), came in and we engaged in what was now becoming a familiar conversation.

'Do you wanna sell the chop?'

'No.'

'But if you were going to sell it, how much would you want?'

Given that I'd paid £350 for what was a £600 motorcycle, I replied. 'I'll take a grand.'

'Here ya go,' said Mark as he counted out the twenties on to my desk.

And with that I helped put it in the back of his truck and he drove off.

Yes, I very much regret selling that bike, and to be honest, I've always wanted another. But if it's any consolation, I'm still sitting on the World of Leather sofas that I bought with the money!

*   *   *

I couldn't possibly list all of the wonderful - and not so wonderful - cars I've had the pleasure to (usually) own and drive, but a couple come to mind. The Chevy El Camino pick-up truck I used to tow the race car in the eighties was a great car - I even raced it once when Rough Diamond was out of action. Back in the days when the tow car would chase the race cars down the track in order to tow them back to the pits, I remember Ron Pudney who was crewing for me one day forgot to put the tailgate up before powering after me - emptying the entire contents of the pick-up bed onto the start line!

An earlier tow-car was the Ford Country Sedan (the one that I parked outside Margaret Thatcher's house). With its roll-down electric window in the tailgate, we used to lay face down on the floor in the back, the driver would activate the electric window, and several bare arses would hoist themselves above the tailgate 'mooning' the cars behind. We thought it was hilarious, most people probably thought it was strange.

We used it to tow the race car to Wroughton one day - it rained all the way there, all the time we were there, and all the way back. I was up front with Dick driving and Dad was in the back, after a while he mentioned that it was getting a bit damp in the back - we ignored him. A little while later he mentioned it again.

'Do you want me to stop, Reg?' Dick asked.

'Well it's lapping round me ankles and my strides are working like a wick,' he replied.

There was about four inches of water in the rear foot-well, and we couldn't work out where or how it was getting in. We punched a couple of drain holes in the floor with a hammer and screwdriver and continued on our way. Dick later bought the car from my dad.

In the period between selling the dragster to Tony, and my buying the Corvette, I managed to build a beach buggy. Our neighbour in West Street had a Beetle up for sale - an MOT failure. Once in our garage, Dad and I made the trek to Fibrefab in Crowthorne who made beach buggy bodies and related parts. I placed an order for a body with its gel-coat finished in Rough

The '10 day' Beach Buggy

Diamond blue, and went back to dismantle the Vee Dub. I stripped it of all the parts I needed, and the body went to the scrap man. We picked up the buggy body shell and assembly began. In only ten days of work over three weeks I had completed beach buggy, and like the Model T before it, it was an absolute blast to drive. I'd have another in a heartbeat.

Another car that was a lot of fun was the Caterham Seven we got in part exchange for the Vauxhall Lotus race car. We asked Neil Melliard to add a yellow flame job on the red body, and I fitted an aero screen. Alli raced it at a couple of sprints and I once entered it at Brighton. With its Dunnell-tuned 2 litre Ford Zetec motor, it was an extremely quick car. I would ultimately put a child seat in it so that I could use it for Scott's school run when he was at primary school.

*   *   *

I intend to get the Rolls re-commissioned, and while the dragster and Dallara are currently unfinished business, I can't see myself racing for much longer. Last year I thought about selling the Harley, but I couldn't bring myself to do it. Another T bucket hot rod however does remain on my 'bucket list' - pun fully intended.

Who knows what the future may bring?

15

Polymathematics in Kent

When we moved from Wallington to East Kent in 2007 I was certain that I'd be able to carry on with my various - albeit reduced - money earning activities. I continued some of the engineering work that I had in what I now refer to as 'The Old Country', but my hope of picking up work locally never came to fruition, and even some of my regular work dropped by the wayside with travel making some things simply not viable.

I continued with the acting work as best I could, but auditions in London were now time-consuming and train travel expensive - I needed to be fairly certain that it was a role that would a) pay well and b) be a job I'd have a good chance of winning. Some of the lower paid corporate video jobs I took were simply not cost effective, and theatre (of which I was probably only ever going to get low paid fringe work), was pretty much out of the question, again due to travel time and costs.

Alli now had her own business consultancy, and was doing well, and as the years went by, work for me evolved. For a while I was less of a polymath than I'd ever been before.

My return to drag racing saw an increase in motor sport related work, building engines and transmissions and so on, which at least I enjoy. I maintained two of my regular engineering customers in 'the old country' but even one of them has now changed hands and moved even further away.

Over the years here in Kent, I'd become friendly with my contact lens optician - a delightful Yorkshire lass called Sally. She'd shared with me that she was getting married, and one day I bumped into her in Sainsbury's and asked how the plans were going. She explained while everything had been organised, her husband-to-be's divorce had not yet come through, and that his father was terminally ill, so they didn't want to cancel as they really wanted him to be there. In order for the ceremony to go ahead she needed - a celebrant.

I'd previously read in a trade magazine about being an independent celebrant, and thought that my skills as a performer might be useful - so looked into it further. However, training was expensive, and I wasn't convinced that there would be a sufficient return on the time and money involved, so I put that idea on the back-burner.

I mentioned that I'd considered being a celebrant, and would be happy to help if I could. Much to my surprise, a couple of days later she got in touch and said that they'd had a chat, and would love for me to be their wedding celebrant. In at the deep end and getting away with it - again.

Mr and Mrs Parrish and virgin celebrant – me!

Sally and Keiron put their complete trust in me, so Google became my friend. I met with them both at the venue, I wrote a ceremony tailored to their needs, and I delivered a service that made the congregation both laugh and cry. And I thought. Blimey, I actually could get away with this!

I subsequently enrolled on a celebrant course and learnt the ropes as they should be done, and I was pleased to discover that I'd done pretty much everything the way it should be. I now had a (further!) qualification to back me up and enrolled in the association which gave me adequate insurance too.

A few months later, her father-in-law Peter, knowing that he had not much time left, asked for me to meet with him so that I could write and conduct his funeral service. He'd enjoyed the wedding enough for him to put his trust in me for his funeral.

Clearly it was an emotional period, but between us we wrote a service with which he was content, and I delivered it as he wished. Fortunately, he was a car guy, with a great sense of humour. One of the songs he chose was '*Leap Up and Down Wave Your Knickers in the Air*' by St Cecilia, and all of the ladies in the congregation were issued with pairs of knickers which they did indeed wave in the air.

With a new string to my polymath bow I set about marketing myself as an independent-family celebrant - just as the Covid-19 pandemic hit.

At much the same time, my good friend Tony Morris, after working in Florida as a carburettor specialist for many years, found himself out of a job and decided to start his own business specialising in race carburettors. And being an Englishman, he'd already built up a loyal following of UK and European racers while working for other carburettor specialists. He decided that he needed a UK agent and invited me to fill that role.

I jumped at the chance, and invested a modest amount in equipment and stock. Working off the back of both our reputations, I immediately had a steady stream of carburettors coming through the workshop - even during lockdown. This is work I sincerely hope will continue long into the future.

This brings us up to date at the time of writing. My polymath tally currently stands at; a little engineering work, some engine building, a race carburettor specialist and an independent celebrant. Perhaps now I can add writer?

Never a dull moment.

16

Location, location, location

I don't really recall anything from living in Muchelney Road, except the previously mentioned vague recollection of my three-year-old self rocking my rocking horse (tube framed, made by Triang down the road in Merton) so hard and fast that I was able to make it go along - something no rocking horse was ever designed to do - along the hall, toward the open front door... and down the front steps - splitting my head open.

Ross Road in Wallington is a different matter. There was of course the 'Big Snow' of nineteen sixty-three, where snow fell non-stop for six weeks - including my sixth birthday. Some of my friends simply couldn't get to my party. One friend who managed to make it was Mike Charman. Mike was in the same class as me at Collingwood Boys School, and lived a few streets away. Mike and I spent a lot of time together as kids, riding our bikes, exploring the woods and parks, and playing on go-karts. We saw less of each other once we got to secondary school - Mike went to Wallington Grammar, I went to Glastonbury. But we kept in touch, and with Mike becoming a talented artist and designer, he was involved in the lettering, paint, and murals on several of my cars. I'm pleased to say we're still in touch sixty years on.

I passed my driving test while I was at Ross Road. I had three lessons in a driving school's Mini Clubman, and I practiced otherwise with Dad in a nineteen sixty-four Chevrolet Impala - I passed first time. It wasn't too long after when we moved to West Street in Carshalton.

The tale of our moving to West Street are detailed elsewhere, but I clearly have fond memories of the cars that both Dad and I owned and the cars that we built. Late nights in the garage were not uncommon, and it was a popular place to visit by my friends - though most of them were scared of my mum. I only had one party that my parents didn't find out about 'til they got back from America - there wasn't too much damage. It was here when I got the call that took me to America, and as you may have read earlier, when I returned from the USA things weren't quite the same as I might have imagined.

When I got back from the USA, Dad was in the throes of converting the Coach House into a dwelling, while selling The Yews and putting the proceeds towards his retirement. What had formerly been a workshop, stores and games room, was in the process of being extended and converted into a two-bedroom detached home, and technically, there wasn't going to be enough room for me.

One late night I was on my way home in the Corvette from... I don't know where, when I pulled up at some traffic lights behind another Corvette, to be precise, another nineteen seventy-eight Silver Anniversary Corvette – identical to mine.

I gave chase.

We ended up in the courtyard of a rather nice private estate of apartments. I can't for the life of me remember the name of the driver and his girlfriend, but it seemed bizarre that he owned the identical car to me, and lived literally around the corner from Mum and Dad. It might have explained why complete strangers had been waving at me - the same had been happening to him!

The couple came from Yorkshire, and were living 'down south' for work. Paula and I (we were dating again), became friendly with them, and when they announced they were to be married, we were invited to their wedding at a rather pleasant hotel in Yorkshire, which I remember was surrounded by a moat and could only be accessed on foot over a small bridge. Of course, we drove there in the 'Vette.

Soon after, they happened to mention that they were moving back to Yorkshire, and their flat was up for sale. At the time Paula and I hadn't really considered moving in together, but the timing was right, I was soon going to be made homeless, so it made all kinds of sense to see if we could afford to buy the flat. And as is often the case, when you make enquiries, you find yourself on an unexpected path.

Thirty-three, Beechwood Court was a good-sized first floor apartment built in the nineteen-thirties, with access to a delightful shared garden, and a full-time caretaker. We made the most of our new home, and decorated accordingly.

Once the relationship with Paula ended, I had a couple of noisy parties (which really pissed off the neighbours), dated Sally for a while, and then Alli moved in. Initially we retained the lodger, but before long we had the place to ourselves. Turning one of the two bedrooms into a dining room transformed it into a very spacious flat.

Alli and I were now married, she had a regular job, and of course I had an irregular income. We were sprinting the Formula Ford which was being kept at my workshop in Hackbridge, but it would have been nice to keep that at home and free up the workspace. We began looking for a house with one absolutely necessary primary requirement - a garage.

We viewed a few potential properties, but we found nothing quite right. Then out of the blue, Alli's parents said they were going to sell their house in Wallington and downsize to a smaller house near Ashford. The timing was perfect. It was a lovely Victorian four-bedroom semi-detached home - a home that Alli had grown up in. We knew the property well and of course trusted the sellers. We sold the flat and bought it.

It didn't have a garage.

Twenty-two Springfield Road - known as Oakhurst - was a lovely place to call home. It possessed many period features, but also many of them had been ripped out by various previous owners. We decorated as best we could afford, returning many of the features that had been lost over time - dado rails, picture rails, and the like. We revealed period floors and carpeted the stairs using stair rods. A proper pull handle bell was installed by the front door, and Neil Melliard hand-painted the name and number in the window above the front door using gold leaf. It was home we were very proud of, it was home we entertained many friends in, it was the home we brought our son home to, it was a home we rented out as a filming location for the television programme *The Bill*.

It still didn't have a garage - or the space in which to build one.

Coincidentally, Oakhurst was just across the road from Collingwood Boys School, the school I went to until I was eleven, and I could see it from my front window. When Scott was just six months old, we signed him up and paid the £50 deposit to be a pupil there once he was old enough - that's how long the waiting list was. We toured the school, and much of it hadn't changed since I went there as a kid. In the meantime, he went to the nursery at the end of the road.

My dad died aged seventy-eight, in 2002. He'd been suffering some renal problems, had a pacemaker fitted, and finally he was taken by pneumonia. Mum passed away four years later, she'd suffered with emphysema for many years, brought on initially by smoking, although it didn't help that she'd had a collapsed lung in her youth.

Most of Alli's family were no longer in the area, and I had no family at all. The area around Wallington and Carshalton was becoming more oppressive, with nearby Croydon and Sutton seemingly invading our space. Noise, dirt and traffic were becoming worse - and we had neighbours. With no reason for either of us to remain in the area, Alli and I decided we could afford to abandon the fifty quid non-returnable deposit we'd given Collingwood School, and 'escape to the country'. But where?

Our main criteria were that easy access to London by train (Alli was regularly having to travel to London), and that what was to become 'the old country' would be about an hour's drive away as I still conducted business in the area. While we were no longer participating in motor sport, we also needed workshop space so that I could work from home, and have somewhere to store some of the collection of vehicles my dad had left me with.

Initially we looked around Crowborough as my old school friend Ian Caple and his family were living there, and we liked the area. But nothing floated our boat. Being familiar with the area around

Lydden where the race circuit was, we stuck a pin in the map and began our search.

We found ourselves driving our Jaguar XJR down a narrow by-way - I was certain there couldn't be anything down here. It was the second of five houses we were due to view that day, and I was sure we'd taken a wrong turn, when after a couple of hundred yards we came upon a cream coloured house and pulled into the yard.

'This'll do,' I said to Alli, before we even got out of the car.

It was more expensive that we could afford (of course), but it met all of our requirements and was the very definition of 'secluded'. We viewed the remaining houses we were booked to view that day, but we knew we were wasting our time.

In March 2007, Chequers Farm, located in an Area of Outstanding Natural Beauty, became our new home. It could have done with a coat of paint inside and out, and frankly fourteen years later much of it still does, but I simply love it here. There are downsides. If you need anything, there's no choice but to drive, and the lanes are filthy and muddy so keeping a car clean is impossible. On the plus side, no-one will be able to build anything in the fields that completely surround us, but then again, we won't be allowed to build anything on our own property. But it has everything I want; a pool, a workshop, and ample parking. However the two and a half acres of grass always seems to need cutting. Alli has her own office in a separate building, Scott has his own study, and I'm blessed with a fantastic view and privacy beyond comparison.

I count my blessings daily.

I'd like to think I'll go out of here in my box, but the reality is we'll probably have to downsize as we get older - I plan on being on this planet for a long time yet!

Epilogue

As I write this we are a year into the coronavirus global pandemic. Scott has barely been out of the house for twelve months, and is missing out on so many things that a fifteen-year-old boy should be experiencing. Not only did we make the decision to enrol him to an online home school (so that he couldn't bring the virus home to us), he has also been a competitive fencer since he was six years old and the Covid-19 situation hasn't allowed for training or competitions. However, he has taught himself to edit video, and has been earning good money editing videos for gamers and podcasters.

Alli has managed to convert all of her work to online, and conducts business and training from her own office. She's been busier than ever, but like Scott, has hardly left our property for the duration of the pandemic.

I've also had plenty of work, albeit only in the engine building and carburettor refurbishment side of things.

With venues closed, the celebrant work has been non-existent. Fellow celebrants are having a dire time of it, and I see no point in trying to promote the venture at this time. Most of the work is found by building relationships with venues - which aren't open, or through wedding fairs - which aren't happening. I'll return to this venture when the time is right.

The long and short of it is that we've not been affected by the pandemic too much; in the grand scheme of things we've been very fortunate, but I know that many people are having a truly horrible time.

*   *   *

As the song says. 'Regrets? I have a few,' and if I had to choose one, it would be not having Scott until after my Dad passed away – he would have been the best Grandad ever.

I've always had a gut feeling that I may have been destined for greater things, but it appears not. Perhaps I should have been less risk-averse when it came to finances, but for me, money has always been too hard to come by to take chances with. Apart from our mortgage, I don't borrow money.

I make no apologies when I say that I am content. I have a wife and son who are well and whom I adore equally. I'm blessed with some good friends and I am extremely fortunate to have what I have, be where I am, and do what I do. I am truly blessed, so perhaps my Mum was right - I do lead a charmed life.

*   *   *

When I began writing this there was no thought of publication, it was primarily with the intention of giving my son some background information, an insight into how we got to where we are - stuff that I never got around to asking my Mum and Dad and wish I had. Things like how they met, and what was life like for them during and after the war. So if you're fortunate enough to have your parents still with you, ask questions, be inquisitive – because they may not tell you otherwise. You never know what you might find out.

*   *   *

If there's any message in all of the preceding it's this, and it's for Scott.

My Dad used to paraphrase the Kipling poem 'If'. 'Though walk with Kings, never lose the common touch', he said. And by this he simply meant, get along with everyone, be someone people want to spend time with, whatever walk of life they are from. If people like you, they will see you well.

But most of all Scott, the best advice I can give you is this. Try not to be a prick.

Follow the Facebook page 'An Accidental Polymath' to view unused images and read the occasional additional recollection – added as and when I find time to recollect and write them.

Printed in Great Britain
by Amazon